GW00546903

BRUTAL SCHOOL TIES

The Parktown Boys'
Tragedy – in the
words of those who
were there

Sam Cowen

mf

Melinda Ferguson Books,
an imprint of NB Publishers, a division of Media24 Boeke (Pty) Ltd
40 Heerengracht, Cape Town, South Africa
PO Box 879, Cape Town 8000, South Africa
www.nb.co.za

Cover design and typography: Wilna Combrinck
Editor: Sean Fraser
Proof reader: Kelly-May Macdonald
Set in Montserrat
Printed and bound by CTP Printers, Cape Town

First published by Melinda Ferguson Books 2020
First edition, first impression

ISBN: 978-1-9284-2100-9
ISBN: 978-1-9284-2101-6 (epub)
ISBN: 978-1-9284-2102-3 (mobi)

"I and the public know
What all schoolchildren learn,
Those to whom evil is done
Do evil in return."
WH Auden, *Collected Poems*

Dedicated to the boys* of Parktown Boys' High School and their families, and Olivia Jasriel.

*Names of the boys and their parents have been changed to protect the identities of the victims.

Contents

Preface

On the night of 3 November, 2016, police arrived at Parktown Boys' High School in Johannesburg, to arrest assistant waterpolo coach, Collan Rex. He had been caught on CCTV camera footage fondling a 15-year-old learner from the boarding house.

In the year that followed, Rex was charged with 327 offences, including 110 counts of attempted murder, 199 of sexual assault, one of rape, two of sexual grooming and eight of assault. There were seven additional charges of "exposure of pornography to a minor". He pleaded guilty to 144 charges of sexual assault and stood trial for the remaining 183.

In November 2018 Rex was found guilty of 144 counts of sexual assault and 12 of common assault. This added up to over 150 years, of which he was sentenced to an effective 23 years in prison.

But that wasn't the end. It wasn't even the beginning.

Prologue

"Let's arrest this monster"

It was a summer evening in early November 2016 and, as is common in Johannesburg at that time of the year, a thunderstorm was brewing. At Druce Hall, the hostel at Parktown Boys' High School, boys were milling around in the dining room, in the quad, and in the television and couch areas. It was a normal Thursday evening, the last night of boarding in the school week. By this time the next day, most of these boys would be watching TV or playing soccer in the garden of their own homes.

Sixteen-year-old boarder, *Jonah, was worried. He had spotted his mother's car in the parking lot, but he hadn't yet seen her. His mind raced. Was he in trouble? Was there something wrong? She hadn't called ahead to say she was coming, and now he was anxious.

Collan Rex, one of the housemasters, stepped outside to stand beside Jonah. Although he was the master in charge of welfare and special events for the hostel, he was young and fun and relatable. He saw himself as more of a friend to the boys than an elder, and they felt much the same about him. He was the guy who inevitably turned a blind eye when they were fooling around instead of knuckling down to their homework during prep time. He was also Jonah's waterpolo coach and they got on really well.

"You okay?" Collan asked.

Jonah wasn't.

"My mom's car is here and she's in with the Bosserts."

Mariolette and Chris Bossert ran the boarding house, he as director and she in the role of matron. Unofficially, she was also the house mom, there for sickness, hot chocolate and sympathy when necessary. The boys adored her.

"Want me to go and ask what's going on?" Collan asked. "I'm sure it's nothing, but I can check for you if you want?"

Jonah nodded.

Collan made his way down to the Bosserts' house. He knocked on the door and Mariolette appeared. The two spoke briefly and he returned to where Jonah was anxiously standing.

"She says it's fine – they're just having a meeting," he said reassuringly. Jonah relaxed.

"It's probably nothing," Collan said as he headed back into the hostel.

It was far from nothing.

Earlier in the evening, the Bosserts had been paid a visit by 16-year-old *Ben. Ben had a problem. He was looking for a bag of waterpolo caps that had been AWOL since Saturday. The team had played a match at the Afrikaanse Hoër Seunskool, affectionately known as 'Affies', and the following day the boys discovered that the waterpolo caps were missing. Ben was sure they had been in the common area at Foundation House when the team returned, but now they were nowhere to be found. The head waterpolo coach had instructed him to find them immediately. Ben suggested they watch the CCTV footage from the day, to see where the caps had gone. Chris Bossert had thus called it up on the big-screen TV in the lounge. He continued marking books, while his wife Mariolette cooked in the kitchen. The couple knew that watching that much footage was going to be really tedious, so they watched with only half an eye, confident that Ben was concentrating on it.

Neither of them remembers now exactly how long the footage had been playing before Ben made a startled sound. Chris was the first to look up. What he saw on the big screen made his blood run cold. There were several boys in the room, sprawled across the couches, playing on their phones and chatting. On a long L-shaped sofa lay a boy, Jonah, in his underwear, his legs across Collan Rex's lap, and Collan was pinching his nipples. Mariolette came running in from the kitchen. The three watched for a few minutes before Chris paused the tape and told Ben to go back to the boarding house and say nothing about this until they had spoken to the boy's mother.

"This is nothing," said Ben. "He does this to all of us, all the time. And more."

Mariolette felt sick. This was the stuff of nightmares.

After sending Ben back to the hostel, she called Jonah's mother, Sharon, and requested that she come to the school immediately. Sharon was anxious –what could possibly be wrong? What could be so bad that they wouldn't tell her over the phone?

She soon found out.

A police van pulled up. Up in their rooms, two of the boys noticed several policemen making their way into the Bosserts' house. No one knew why they were there. Upstairs, Collan himself was chatting to his roommate, entirely oblivious as to what was happening just metres away.

The Bosserts showed the police the footage. Mariolette's hands were trembling. It seemed to go on and on; further into the tape, other boys became involved, the nightmare never ending. The cops were horrified.

"Come, let's arrest this monster," said Officer *Tabane.

Collan was lying on his bed when the door opened and Chris Bossert came in, a strange look on his face. Collan knew instantly that something was wrong.

"Pull some long pants on and get whatever you need ... then come," said Chris.

On the way out, they spotted Mariolette. She was crying.

"Wat het ek gedoen?" asked Collan.

"You know exactly what you did," she wept.

Collan stood next to the police van, smoking, while Chris and the policeman remained inside, deciding what to do next. The two boys were still watching from the upstairs window. They should have been asleep hours ago – there was an exam to write in the morning – but they weren't going to miss this for anything.

Eventually, Collan climbed into the back of the van, the officers shut the door behind him and the police drove off. He didn't know it, but this was the last time Collan Rex would ever see Parktown Boys'.

Chapter 1
Normalising the Abnormal

"You have to see the video."

"I don't want to see the video," I said firmly.

"You have to see it to understand why it was so horrific." Olivia Jasriel was just as firm. I have enormous respect for Olivia – she is one of the bravest women I know. Having survived being raped and abused by convicted paedophile tennis champ, Bob Hewitt, she has become a tireless campaigner for the rights of victims of sexual abuse.

We had just finished an interview for a series I was compiling about women who had overcome trauma and tragedy. Olivia had spoken about what had happened to her, and why, over 20 years later, she had risked so much to bring her rapist to justice.

"You know, I still bath in bleach," she had said during the interview.

Hewitt had raped her when she was 12. She had recently turned 50.

"Even now?" I asked.

"Yes, even now. Sometimes a cupful, sometimes a capful and then I scrub and scrub."

She smiled sadly. "But maybe one day I will just have to smell it."

After the interview, she brought up the Parktown Boys' case. "You should talk to some of the moms, get their stories."

I shook my head.

"I'm not going to call up any mother and say, 'Hi, sorry your son was molested, wanna do an interview?"

She frowned. "You'd never do that."

"No, I'd never do that. But the case is over, isn't it?"

This was August 2019. Rex had been sentenced in November 2018.

"The case is over, sure ... but these moms are hurting, Sam. I was with some of them the other day. Their sons are still so broken. They've been forgotten and betrayed. And it's far from over."

I stopped and looked at her.

"What do you mean it's far from over?"

"The initiation and everything ... it's all still going on."

"But this wasn't initiation."

From what I had read, the abuse had taken place at the hands of the waterpolo coach and only in the hostel.

"It starts there. It gets normalised there."

"What do you want me to do?" I really didn't know.

"Speak to Luke Lamprecht. The system needs to be exposed."

Luke is a tireless fighter in the war against child abuse. He had supported Olivia throughout the Hewitt trial and subsequent parole hearings. And he had been involved in the Rex case.

"Ask him to show you the video."

"There was a video?"

How horrific, I thought. I didn't want to see that. I didn't even want to think about what was on that tape.

"Please speak to Luke, Sam. Please."

I love Olivia, so I called Luke.

We met at Doppio Zero in Greenside a few weeks later. He arrived, a ball of energy. Intense. Even sitting down, Luke is never still.

"What do you know about the case?" he asked.

What I had read in the papers, I told him. The case had been very well covered and I now knew a lot more about it. I would later hear that Rex had had more charges against him than anyone else in South African history. I wasn't sure how true that was, but he faced 327 – a number I battled to grasp. Even the judge, Peet Johnson, was thrown. At the sentencing, he stated that he'd never before come across a case in which a person was found guilty of so many sexual assault counts. "From the facts, you cannot be described in any other way but a serial sexual offender and sexual bully," he had pronounced.

Rex sounded like a monster.

Luke nodded. "He's where he should be."

"Tell me about the tape," I asked.

He raised an eyebrow.

"Olivia says that if I want to understand the true horror of it, I need to see the tape."

There was a pause.

"Is it very brutal?" I asked. "Is that what it is?"

He shook his head.

"No, not ... brutal."

"Then what?"

"You can't unsee something like that."

I was impatient.

"Look, I'm not going to see it at all. I just want to know why it's so terrible."

Luke took a sip of his drink and then looked me full in the face.

"Because of the normality of it ... There are a few boys in the room and while Rex is molesting one, others are coming in and out and laughing and joking. And then he molests another one and so it continues."

"Is he doing it behind a door or something?" I asked, still not getting it.

"No. It's in the open. He had been doing it for so long that they just accepted it as normal."

That's terrible, I thought.

"Let's meet when I get back from New York," Luke said. Later he sent me the numbers of people he thought might talk to me. One of those showed me the tape.

It begins with what I suppose is a typical scene in the common area of a boys' school. One boy lies on a couch off to the right of the screen, engaged with something on his smartphone. Collan Rex is sprawled across an L-shaped sofa in the middle of the room, watching something on his phone. The CCTV camera has him in the centre of the frame. After a few minutes, another boy enters the room. Rex says something to him and the boy starts to take off his clothes. When he is down to his underpants, he comes and sits on the long side of the L, his legs over Rex's lap. For a few minutes, nothing happens, all three on their phones. Then Rex's hand starts moving up and down the boy's leg. Up and down. Up and down. Creeping closer and closer to the edge of his boxer briefs. It seems almost a natural progression when his hand eventually slips inside and stays there. His hand is still moving when another two boys enter the room to talk to him. He doesn't pull his hand away immediately. No one raises an alarm, or even seems shocked or surprised at what is happening. The second boy on the couch to the right hasn't moved. Finally, Rex pulls his hand out from under the briefs, rests it gently on the boy's legs for a moment and then starts fondling his nipples. The whole scene seems so frighteningly 'normal': boys continue to move in and out of the camera frame, no one points or shouts or appears in any way concerned. I would hear later that this was the Rex way.

I managed about five minutes, maybe 10. It felt like a lifetime.

Luke was right. I would never, ever be able to unsee it. I drove away from that knowing that I would never be the same again.

What seeing it did do, however, was fuel a mighty rage, a rage at a monster who preyed on young boys. Rage at a school system that allowed it to happen, and rage that these boys who had come forward so bravely were now broken and suicidal and sad and shamed. At that point I thought I would be writing a book about a group of heroes and a villain. Before I was halfway through, I realised that most of the monsters still walked free. Their victims less so.

Chapter 2
The Archivist
*Ben's father

For a long while I relied only on what Luke had told me, my own fleeting glance at the footage, and a paper trail of parents' and newspaper reports. It was very difficult to pin down details I could trust. Someone told me Collan had been beaten to a pulp in jail, with others backing up the story. Then I discovered it was all just a rumour. I was told one of the boys had committed suicide, and, yes, there had been suicides, but years earlier and nothing to do with the current issue or school management team. It was extremely frustrating. And worrying.

Enter the Archivist. I had been wanting to talk to him for some time. He was Ben's father. Ben the whistleblower, the boy who had alerted the Bosserts about the CCTV footage of Rex groping Jonah and other boys in the common area. He had only been in Grade 10 at the time, and I was stunned at the bravery of this 16-year-old in bringing it into the open. Father and son had been on some podcasts and radio shows, talking about what had happened to Ben at school at the hands of Collan Rex. Listening to him and his dad, I was struck by two things: the closeness they shared and the openness with which Ben was prepared to talk about the details of the case, and himself in particular. I wanted to speak to both of them.

What I didn't know when I first messaged Ben's father was that he was the unofficial archivist of the entire case. Over months of conversations and debates about what to include and what not, he was the one I went to again and again, when I needed to check what someone had said or claimed, or when dates seemed wrong. He had kept records of everything – from documents to videos to audio recordings. There was nothing this man did not know or could not find out, and he became, for me, a person of trust.

"Do you think Ben would speak to me?" I asked him.

"Yes, I do," he said. "One of the things I've tried to do – and I think it's helped – is get him to talk about it. It's part of his healing, part of his recovery."

Ben was away at the time and the Archivist wanted to see me to clarify things before he would allow me to meet his son.

"I would like to meet with you and have a conversation. Partly about what you're doing and being a part of it, but also because I would like to ... explain Ben to you."

"Is he okay?"

Every time I asked that of someone, I was struck with the stupidity of the question. How could anyone be okay after something like that?

I'd been in contact with Sasha-Lee Olivier that month; she'd been crowned First Princess in Miss South Africa that year and had eventually taken over the title after the winner had won Miss Universe. In a bid to help raise awareness for childhood victims, she was starting to talk about her own abuse as a child, and when I asked her when she'd become okay to talk about it, she was quiet for a while.

"I became okay about talking about it when I realised I would never be okay about talking about it," had been her response.

I told that story to all those I interviewed. It was an icebreaker. And it really worked.

"Yeah, he's okay," said the Archivist. "But I want to talk to you first and tell you some stuff you may or may not know and after that, you can meet him."

So, on a very hot afternoon towards the end of 2019, I sat down with Ben's father and his wife at their home and he told me "some stuff". Actually, he told me "lots of stuff".

The Archivist is a big man and fairly intimidating in person. At that point, I was still quite nervous of this gatekeeper of the information. I told him what I knew and how it made me feel. I told him about looking at the first few minutes of the video and what had horrified me – and he stopped me right there.

"I actually chose not to see the footage," he said. "I've been offered it several times, and told that I need to see it, and I don't want to see it. I've heard more or less what it's about. And, yes, what stopped Rex – or, rather, Ben revealing it in the way he did was what stopped Rex. But, from my perspective, it's also something that I feel I don't need to see and that I don't want to see. I feel for these kids when I see them and I know them, but I don't want to have them know that I've seen it and have them have to deal with the worry that this guy knows what happened. So that's the reason I chose not to see it, and it also keeps me level-headed. I get upset quite easily, lose my temper about that kind of thing."

So does Ben – Ben gets it from him, he says.

"I sat right behind Rex in court and I was, to be honest, looking for a confrontation, if he wanted that. And I suppose also I just wanted to stand up to him, but not really to fight him, just to show him that 'I'm not afraid of you.'"

"But you didn't."

"No, I didn't."

"Did you ever suspect anything? Did Ben ever say anything to you before the video?"

This was the watershed moment for many. Before and after the video.

"So, Ben came to me and he said that during training they would play no-rules waterpolo where they rough each other up and push each other down, just to toughen them up and get them not to panic while it's happening in a real game kind of thing. And he said that Rex had grabbed his balls. I think it was as simple as that."

"And were you worried?" I asked.

"I told him that that kind of thing happens in sport, like when playing soccer. So that's what I dismissed it as."

He looked sad for a minute.

"I guess I have to live with that."

"You could never have known," I said.

"Yeah, but then Ben changed a bit. Although he kept it quiet, he started getting a little more aggressive and harder because he was becoming a harder boy."

"I've heard Collan was very rough with the boys, and wrestled with them a lot, as well as the other stuff," I said.

"Ben had many incidents in the hostel, fighting and obviously making a noise ... The ones that stand out, I suppose, involved wrestling. Ben said that Collan would frequently come into the room and fight with him. And Collan would also lift Ben's legs up above the head and dry hump him – that was something he did regularly, while in a wrestling match. So he'd come in looking for wrestling and end up doing something like that. He'd put their legs over his shoulder, so that he'd ... I suppose get a better angle, I guess, I don't know. But he had that habit of doing that to the boys. In one instance, Ben

21

went on tour to Durban with Rex, and there were a few incidents that took place there. One was when Ben came into a room where another boy was being dry humped, so Ben kicked Rex off this kid, and Rex got up and chased him down. He grabbed him and put him into some sort of a leg-lock, where he had Ben between his legs and choked him until Ben passed out. And there were other kids around – in fact, I heard one kid filmed it. But his parents didn't want him getting involved so they apparently deleted it."

"So it was more in fun than an actual desire to hurt them?" I asked, "because I've heard this from a few of the boys and even their parents and so I wondered why the prosecutor charged him with so many counts of attempted murder. And then the judge pretty much dismissed them anyway."

He nodded.

"Ja, rightfully so – it wasn't attempted murder. He never intentionally tried to kill them. The prosecution would have had more success if they had just made it common assault and made a few that were more severe, with grievous bodily harm. But the wrestling and stuff was fairly common ... very common. Ben, in this case when he got knocked out. Also later on that tour ... I don't know how far apart the incidents were ... but on the same tour, he shared a shower, not the same actual shower, but within the location there were two shower heads, and he was sharing that with Rex. Rex tried to grab his bum, but Ben told him to fuck off and leave him alone. Rex's response was to urinate on Ben, and Ben then retaliated by urinating on Rex. And this is the thing ... for Ben and a lot of the boys, it became a way of bantering, of having a fight. I think the reason it felt all right, in my opinion, was that they were invited to do the same, if you know what I mean. So when he grabbed them, he poked them, then it would be okay, like Ben would occasionally get an advantage over him and choke him, and grab his balls and squeeze his whatever. So it became like a banter thing, where eventually the boys started doing it to each other because it appeared as though it was fine to do. I don't know if Rex intended for things to go as far as they did eventually, but this type of banter may even be how he got involved in the whole thing in the first place; it may have happened to him, so that whole back-and-forth became more of an accepted behaviour."

"When did that acceptance of it 'being normal' stop for Ben?" I really wanted to know.

"When Ben started realising it was a problem, was when the new boys came in and they were very upset by it happening to them. Ben started noticing that. He became more concerned about his fellow students, particularly the younger boys. Ben had a very strong sense of brotherhood when it came to Parktown Boys, and he still has that. He feels responsible, he takes blame, he was the kind of kid that if somebody did something wrong, he would own up to it to protect them. And I think that had a lot to do with him coming forward to try to stop what was happening."

"Your son is very brave," I said. "He put a monster behind bars."

The Archivist smiled ruefully.

"You know, Ben didn't want that. He just wanted to get Rex fired, that's what he said. He wanted it to stop. It was after that Durban tour that Ben decided that he needed to do something about it. I think it was either the first or second game they played, after returning from that tour, that Ben decided. Apparently, Rex was busy with a couple of boys at the back of the bus, where he was doing stupid things, grabbing them and their genitals and stuff, and Ben obviously heard what was going on. So when they all got off the bus, he saw that Rex was going to the common area with a few boys, and Ben knew what usually happened there and that he would be able to get footage, because a camera had been installed there. He wasn't there when it actually happened; I'd actually fetched him that day, but in his mind he was busy dealing with it. He thought of a way to do it … to report the waterpolo caps missing. They weren't actually missing – he knew where they were. So I think that was his thought process; he would report the caps missing and then the Bosserts would watch the footage of what was going on between Rex and the boys in that common area."

And that's exactly what happened.

Ben took the footage to the matron and her husband. He made a loud noise to draw their attention to the part where Rex was molesting a boy. And Rex was arrested. Parents of victim boys were called. But not all of them were on board to take any action.

"Were there repercussions afterwards?"

"We had numerous meetings with parents. The parents would sit and debate whether or not they should continue, because they were concerned about dragging their kids through this. My point of view was: actually, it's quite simple, right now your kid might not be going through what he needs to go through, but I'd rather be in a position 10 years from now, having my son know that I've done everything I possibly could to fight for him, as opposed to my son realising that I didn't do anything to fight for him, when I had the opportunity. So I tried desperately to get parents to back their kids on everything, but there were those parents who pulled out. Like the one kid who had filmed the footage – his parents said, 'Don't get involved.' He'd actually put together a statement of stuff that had happened to him but he had to withdraw. So he was a victim, but they completely pulled him out. Then several other victims withdrew from the whole process."

I wondered what the long-term impact of that would be. The Archivist read my mind.

"What could come back to bite them is when they start to resent their parents for not having acted. But the good thing about their recovery is that the success of the case will give them some sort of relief to know that it was wrong and that Rex has been punished. But the long and the short of it, though, is that the school, I feel, is responsible not for what he did, but for creating an environment where this behaviour was possible. And that's what needs to change."

"So already Ben was up against something he probably didn't expect," I said, "because you'd think parents would want the man who molested their kids to go to jail for a long time. I would. And for every child who testified, that could mean another year."

The Archivist nodded.

"I believe Rex was arrested on 3 November and after that all the kids involved had to write a statement. There was a meeting at the school with the kids, parents, teachers and people on the committee. But the kids weren't speaking, because they were mostly younger, mostly in Grade 8. They were denying that anything had happened. They said, 'No, no, nothing happened, nothing.' So Ben asked the adults, the parents and teachers to leave the room so he could encourage the kids to open up about what had happened to them.

"They all left the room but stood outside listening at the window. Ben started talking to the boys; he said, 'Okay, this has happened to me,' and he started explaining what had happened to him. And then he started pointing at certain boys and said, 'I know this happened to you, I know this happened to you, I know this happened to you.' And he started going through everybody and he said, 'We have to do something about this.' So he basically got all of them to start talking. Once they – I think, because they were mostly younger than him – once they saw this whole respect thing and that one of their older brothers was making a stand, they started to open up more about it."

"That's incredible," I said. I meant it.

The Archivist sighed.

"Problem is that they got the boys into some kind of group therapy with a so-called counsellor or therapist, and she told them stuff that I don't think was told to them the right way. The advice that she gave was quite simply that, 'you deserve respect and if you don't get it, you should fight for it,' – which was stupid advice because it wasn't delivered properly.

"Soon afterwards we started having a very hard time with Ben. Any sort of confrontation, any sort of disagreement, or when he felt that he was being treated badly, turned into 'But why don't you respect me?' I said, 'But, Ben, you need to respect us – we're your parents, my boy.' And he would say, 'Ja, but you need to respect me.'

"Ben was a tough kid; he was strong, he was not scared – he could take you on physically. And I think his aggression and his spiral could have been prevented if [the therapist] wasn't around. It certainly put Ben in a bad space. As a result, because his brotherhood was important to him, he started fighting for everyone because he felt that they couldn't fight for themselves.

"In class once there were three boys who were told to stand because they were sitting in the wrong place, and the teacher basically told them to stand for the whole lesson. The boys were black students. Ben lost his shit and actually confronted the teacher and gave him a lecture; he said that the teacher was at fault because he had moved one of the desks in the class and that had made it unclear as to where they were meant to be sitting. The teacher reported Ben's outburst to the grade head and later returned to the class. The lesson ended and Ben went to speak to the teacher; he was still adamant that the teacher was at fault. The teacher started pushing Ben and Ben told him not to touch him. The teacher pushed him again and Ben reacted instinctively and threw him onto a table ... Obviously, that didn't turn out well. The teacher reported him again. I had a meeting with Mr Derek Bradley, the principal at the time, and I said that Ben had been standing up for his brothers, and that I had felt that it may have been a race issue, and Ben had dealt with it. I said to the principal that I tried to explain to Ben that this could have been dealt with very differently, and that he should have taken his concerns to the principal or asked me to take this to the principal. Eventually that teacher apologised to Ben for his actions and Ben apologised to him, and there were no further repercussions. But it did form part of future encounters when that incident was brought up and people would say, 'Ben's got no respect.' that kind of thing."

Ben's mother had come into the room during our conversation.

"We didn't know everything that had happened to him at that

point, so it was quite difficult because we had to get him to write down dates and details: when it started, which camps, trying to get everything in order. He sat with my husband for a long time writing that out. We didn't know, for example, all of what had happened from Grade 8. And the more he told us, the more things we found out. And it just got worse and worse. His anger every weekend just got worse and worse. His friendships almost immediately changed; he started hanging out with the wrong boys – well, some of them anyway. When he exposed Rex, a lot of kids turned against him, many of whom were his peers, in the sense that they were the waterpolo players and rugby players; he lost friendships with a lot of the boys, because he had been the source of the information. So he became the scapegoat and the snitch. And they have this thing at Parktown: 'You snitch, you die' and 'Snitches get stitches'."

The Archivist joined in.

"The problem is that Ben's fairly honest – even if it's not immediately, he tells us the truth. He told us that he and a few other boys had been caught with drugs by Mariolette and that they'd begged her and Chris not to say anything. In the hostel, he and a couple of kids would get out the school, walk to Braamfontein and buy all kinds of drugs. They smoked a lot of weed; I think 11pm was lights out and they would all smoke in their room, open the window. And then Mariolette and Chris started realising what was going on – the victim kids were doing drugs. She took them to some sort of drug rehab in town, and they all had to have urine tests. Ben spat on his test. But the drugs just kept getting worse and worse."

The Archivist's wife was nodding.

"I really struggled. I had been in a clinic for three weeks because of the stress and when I came back, things were worse. Ben was drinking, taking drugs; he would go to clubs in the middle of town, but in like, really dodgy areas and his aggression was out of hand. Once his dad had to go and fetch him from the hostel because he was so drunk. He woke up here the next morning and had no idea how he had got here."

Dad was nodding.

"The fact that he walked – because I'm not going to carry anybody – to the car and then up the stairs, got into bed, and he had no recollection of it ... that was worrying."

His wife continued.

"Ben punched doors, punched walls, screamed, like really screamed at us, I actually got scared."

The Archivist added: "He'd also sit there, trying to get me to fight him. He would say, "Hit me, why don't you hit me? Hit me.' And I wouldn't. I just wouldn't."

"Then he would say he loves fighting," said Ben's mom. "He absolutely loves it. And it all got too much for me. I felt responsible to a certain degree, so did my husband, because he's at this school and we never knew what was going on. But then he tried to commit suicide and we had to focus on that."

"What?" I was stunned.

The Archivist nodded his head.

"One night Ben tried to jump off a bridge near Ontdekkers and Gordon Road onto the highway ... I don't actually remember what led to it, but he got out of the car in frustration and I wasn't going to say, 'Well, sorry, get back in the car.' His twin brother wanted to calm him down, but I said to him, 'Just leave him. Let him walk home – he knows where he lives.' It was bloody far away from there, but he knew where we lived. His brother insisted. He got out of the car and chased Ben while I stayed in the car, following as they went around corners, close enough, but keeping my distance so that Ben would stop running away. Eventually his twin called me and shouted, 'Ben's going to jump off the bridge!' So I said, 'Whatever you do, do not tell him not to jump.' Ben is not scared – he has no fear, nothing – so if he said to Ben, 'You're not going to jump off that bridge,' he would have jumped. I said, 'Ask him what he wants to do ... What does he want me to do?' His twin said Ben wanted to go to his girlfriend's house. I said, 'Cool, I'll drop him there.' But that broke his brother – he was in tears. We decided then to send Ben to Beethoven Clinic near Hartbeespoort Dam, which is where my wife had been earlier in the year."

"How did you manage," I asked, "with your wife in hospital and your son on the absolute edge?"

"In a way, it was easier to manage because my wife was *really* affected by it. It was also about trying to manage her expectations and also trying to keep her in a good space, so having her there was a comfort in a sense that I felt like she was in a good space."

I could understand that. It's hard enough watching one person you love, suffer. Two must have been agony.

His wife interjected.

"So Ben went to Beethoven – and it was just before his matric exams, which was another concern. I spent hours, and I mean hours, trying to get Ben to write his matric at Hartbeespoort Hoërskool. I tried to get them firstly to go to Beethoven and just have somebody watch him. They agreed to that and then said no. We eventually got permission for him to write his exams at Hartbeespoort Hoërskool. But it was such a mission, and we were so worried about how we were going to get him there in the morning. Eventually my husband spoke to a teacher who fetched him and dropped him off. But, I mean, the days he would write, I would phone him in the morning, and ask him, 'Are you okay?' But he was so drugged up. I don't know what they gave him there. He was on 14 different medications; he was taking 26 tablets a day. He sounded drunk from morning to night."

In a way, he was.

"He was supposed to go for 21 days. So they did the drug rehab for 21 days, they did psych for another 21 days and he then stayed longer, so he was there for 52 days all in all. He wrote all of his exams there. He very nearly failed matric. When the results first came out, it looked as though Ben had failed Maths by one per cent and he failed, I think, Business by three per cent. So we asked for a remark on both subjects and fortunately he ended up passing his Maths. So that was matric – he passed ... but only just."

"How did he manage in court?"

Ben is the only boy who was required to testify as an adult. By the time the case came to trial, he was 18 so, even though he had been molested as a minor, he was now considered an adult and had to face his attacker in the courtroom. He wasn't in a separate room like the others. He had to face Collan head-on.

"He coped very well," The Archivist replied, "especially in the face of how the judge behaved with regards to the assault charges. Ben took the stand and he was interrogated by the defence attorney about how he had come to the total of 20 incidents of common assault. The defence asked him things like: 'How do you know it was 20 times? How do you know this was happening? And do you have the exact dates? And what did he do? Weren't you just fighting with each other?'

"Then the judge got involved and said, 'But how do you get to 20?' So Ben said, 'It was more than 20 times.' The judge then said, 'Do you know the dates it took place?' Ben said no. The judge continued, 'But how do you know it was 20?' Ben started trying to explain how he had come to that figure, but the judge said to him that he had to know the dates when the incidences happened. Then I interrupted the judge and said, 'Just listen!' He then said to me, 'You keep quiet!' So I said, 'No, just give him a chance to explain. You asked him – now let him explain!'

"The judge then said he would have me removed from court, but after that, he didn't give me any more shit. So he asked Ben again and Ben said that it had happened over a period of time and that it had been more than 20, but 20 would have been a safe estimate. He said he didn't want to say it was 50 because that might have been too much. The judge then said, 'You can't do that.' But when they questioned Rex, and they asked him if he disputed what Ben had said, Rex said, 'No'. However, the judge then decided he'd take those 20 charges and make them into one. He did this with all the boys, made all their assaults just one. I felt this was ridiculous because Rex had not disputed the numbers. If the accused says, 'I agree with you, there you go, tick, tick, tick, done,' you don't have to sit and play around with it any more."

"What was the worst part of the case for you?" I asked.

Both the Archivist and his wife were at one with their answers: when the charges were read out in court.

Ben's dad explained: "We weren't prepared. The prosecution didn't give us any indication of what was going to happen. We had assumed from what she had said and also what we understood from Ben, that she was going to say 20 or around 20 charges, just because there weren't exact dates. But when she read out the charges, some of which involved Ben, we sat through 20 and then it went on to 30 and then 40 and 50 and eventually there were 144 counts of sexual assault to which Rex pleaded guilty and 57 of them were related to my son. Fifty-seven! And even then I thought to myself, well, if it's 57, it's probably more, because I know how he'd worked out the assault charges, which got condensed from 20 (definitely more) down to one."

The Archivist gave his wife a weak smile.

"I don't know why Rex pleaded guilty to so many. The judge initially looked as though he was siding with the defence, so when Rex pleaded guilty or acknowledged his actions for the 144 charges, I thought he was looking for favour with the judge in that if he acknowledged some wrong, then he wouldn't be found guilty of the stuff that he hadn't acknowledged. I basically thought it was a defence tactic ... Then the judge said to him, 'You doing this is essentially pleading guilty to all those charges.' And Rex said he understood that."

"How do you feel now," I asked, "a year on from the verdict?"

The Archivist shrugged.

"My biggest concern is obviously Ben, but besides that, my problem is that it's something that could have been prevented. At the moment there's a lot of people who don't seem to want to address that. I'm not involved at all in the school any more, but apparently nothing's changed – it's still carrying on. And, for me, that's just stupid. It doesn't make any sense at all. That's what I battle with – the stupidity of it. But the long and the short of it, is that I feel the school is responsible, not just for what Rex did, but for creating an environment where it was possible. And that's what needs to change. But apparently now it's just exploding.

"Ben is now in Somalia working on a rig. He went down to Cape Town and did a rope access course and he's also done water rescue and emergency stuff. He's done a few courses. He loves it. He's very physical and it's hard work and it keeps him busy. He's finally, only now, doing what he wants to do."

I thanked the Archivist and his wife.

But before I left he asked, "Do you need documents or recordings? I have pretty much everything. I record everything, phone calls, a lot of what happened in court. The sentencing, even the report summaries."

He was a gold mine. He still is.

Chapter 3
The Boy Who Blew The Whistle
*Ben

I had read a lot about Ben before I actually met him. Ben, The Archivist's son, who had exposed Collan Rex by getting the hostel director and his wife to look at the CCTV footage. I wondered whether his action had been deliberate or, as one of the other boys would go on to tell me, just lucky. Ben stood out from all the others boys because he had been the one to stop it. Of the 144 sexual charges to which Collan Rex pleaded guilty, his name was listed on 57 of them, the most by almost double. He was the one who had encouraged other boys to testify, and the one who had to face Rex in court.

Ben had also been a guest on a podcast with his dad and he had used his real name. He was very open about what had happened, what had been done to him and what he had done about it. He was happy enough to do the same for this book, but I wanted to give him the option.

"If you use your own name, this will be with you forever. If you use another name, if you decide in 10 years' time that you want nothing to do with this, that you've moved on, no one needs to know. And if you want only certain people to know, you can show them the book and say, see this? I am Ben."

After chatting to the Archivist, Ben agreed with me. They are very close, Ben telling me on more than one occasion that he wanted to be just like his dad.

I went to see them both at home. The Archivist had said that his son was a physical person and I picked up on that immediately. Ben moved around a lot during the conversation. He was good-looking, with that added benefit of youth and vitality. He reminded me of a coiled spring. He was also extremely sure of himself, quite different to other boys I spoke to, some of them having blocked stuff out, some still wrestling with the guilt and the shame. Ben had done a lot of hard work processing that already, and, he said, it had helped that he had talked about it so much.

"When did you decide you were going to expose Collan Rex?" I asked.

"After the last waterpolo tour down to Durban," he said. "Something happened that just made me say, 'enough is enough'."

"Why? What happened in Durban?" I asked.

The Archivist shook his head.

"First you need to understand what happened leading up to it."

Ben laughed. He knew what was coming.

"Start at the beginning, bud," said his father.

And, of course, the beginning was the Grade 8 camp.

"Well, the big thing was that if you wanted to go to the school you had to become a man. So that's basically what the camp was about. At 13, you don't know anything, and no one wants to tell you anything about it. They just say, 'Wait until you get there,' so you know it's going to be a rat hole, you know it's going to be hard, but whatever, you prepare yourself. And I was willing to do it, if it was the only thing that would get me to be accepted, I guess. So then when we got there … actually it started one day before that, in the hostel. If you were a boarder, you had to get to hostel a day earlier and you had to do a whole initiation thing. All the Grade 8s had to stand on a chair, and they asked you questions, just to try to make you feel uncomfortable. Anyway, on the first day of camp we did push-ups until whatever time at night and then someone broke a bed and so we had to get up again and it just carried on with push-ups, and running around. Then there weren't enough beds, so me and my friend didn't get a bed for the first night. The second night, I think we found a mattress or something, so that was fine.

"And on another day, one of the counsellors at the farm where we were, went down to the river and did some activities and made rafts, and one of the oke's shoes fell out of a bag into the water, but we didn't see it, so we just carried on, going on the raft. Eventually we came back for lunch. The oke started shouting, 'Someone threw my shoe in the water!' He got all irritated, and said, 'You better own up.' And then the matrics decided that we had to find the shoe or everyone was going to be punished. So I just said, 'Stuff it,' and I stood up and I said, 'Sorry, sir, it was me who chucked the shoe in the water.' I did this because then only one person was going to do punishment. It stopped everyone else from getting punished."

That was quite something, I thought. Noble and stupid but also possibly dangerous. I'd heard enough in my other interviews by now, to know what those matrics were capable of. But I had to remind myself that, at that time, Ben had no idea who he was dealing with.

"I was taken aside and had to run against a quad bike, and basically drop down, do push-ups, carry on running, drop down, do push-ups, carry on running ... Ja, and that just carried on for a long time. I don't know why they did it; trying to teach me to grow up, I guess, I don't know.

"That night we had to sleep on the grass and one of the matrics came and started whacking everyone awake with a stick. Then we had to run down a hill and do a whole fitness thing every morning. The main thing they tried to teach us was that if one person doesn't do something right, everybody pays for it. So if someone wasn't doing a sit-up properly ... they would just make us keep on going until everyone did it properly. And I think that's when everyone started to learn what was going on, that if anyone does something wrong, everyone pays for it, and if it's you, then everyone hates you. In their opinion, that's how you got everyone in shape. So you try not to do anything wrong, otherwise everyone hates you. And 'snitches get stitches'. They said, 'You tell on us, and everyone's going to hate you.'"

"And do they?" I asked.

"Yes. Yes, they do."

Chapter 4
The Boy with the Marks on his Back
James

Mariolette Bossert held a special place in her heart for *James. James was sweet and soft and he had been badly abused, not just by Collan, but by the matrics too. He was just one of the boys who contemplated suicide.

"He is so special, Sam," said Mariolette. "I just want to protect him so much."

And when I met him, I understood what she meant. He was quiet and thoughtful and very vulnerable. He sat with a small dog on his lap, and throughout the entire conversation, it kept looking up at him with concern. Dogs really are the only animals that can have your back without making a sound.

"He said to me that if his mom had been alive, she would never have let him go to Parktown and those things would never have happened," Mariolette wept. Later, I wept too.

"In Grade 8," said James, "I thought the hostel seemed okay then because the housemaster promoted it as a nice place, but it went downhill from there. You'd think the teachers would be caring, but I felt like they didn't really care and ignored stuff that was done to you. Like, sometimes the teachers would just tell the matrics off, and sometimes they would just ignore stuff and let it happen and I don't know how I feel about that.

"I couldn't say anything to my father because if I did, he would have gone to the school and then everyone would have found out that it was me who had told, that I was a snitch. The masters back then would name and shame you. And the boys, they would make you feel ashamed for telling. If you told, you weren't going to be part of them any more and they would leave you out of everything. It was hard to decide whether to make friends there by saying nothing, or say something and not have friends.

"Some of the matrics were okay – they were chilled out – but other matrics made you feel uncomfortable; they asked you questions like what kind of porn you watched. I'm not comfortable talking about what else they asked.

"They would try out stuff that would be painful and uncomfortable. Like, you know that machine they use in physiotherapy for your muscles? They would put it on our cheeks and turn it on. They put it on my cheeks and one boy's privates. It hurt like hell. We couldn't say anything back then, so we had to just keep silent the whole time.

"In Grade 8, I was planning on committing suicide at the beginning of the year. I was so shocked by how the hostel people lied to me about how it was, and I couldn't take how they treated me in hostel any more, how my peers treated me and how all the other grades treated me.

"On your birthday, you had to stand on a chair in the dining hall and sing 'Happy Birthday' to yourself. And you also got wedgies. So I didn't let anyone know when my birthday was that year. Which made it kind of not special. The things that my old pot [matric mentor] did to me ... He was mostly cool and stuff, until one time I failed in my report. He took a cricket bat and hit me 11 times with it on the butt. It hurt worse than a devil poking you with his fork. I was sore the whole night. It happened towards the beginning of the week, so by the weekend the bruises had faded. There were two old pots per Grade 8, and the other one hit me once because I didn't do well that term. I didn't do good at all because it was first time I'd ever written mid-year exams and you wouldn't expect them to happen so early. But he could have just told me to stay on my game, instead of hitting me. I was scared about the next time I failed; I was really scared.

"I couldn't take it any more so I decided I was going to kill myself. I didn't know what else I was going to do. But I just realised this: if I committed suicide, what about the people I would leave behind, like my dad? He had no one else, he had no one else ... My mother had died just before then and if I died he would have no one.

"I miss my mom a lot. It was ridiculous how people insulted her at the beginning of the year. Some people said, 'She died because she was sick of you.' I lost her when I was in Grade 5, but you can't change the past. I was in a very dark place back then, losing a person who I had so much in common with. We played games together; she did care. My dad, we don't have that much in common. It's hard to think

36

about her sometimes.

"I was an easy target back then. I was quiet. No one noticed I was there most of the time; when people did notice, they were very surprised because I was like a ghost. But there were times I was driven over the edge. Once when I was in Grade 8 I broke a broom over someone's leg. I was shocked at myself. It was the constant bullying and insults. Every night before I went to bed, I would hear the insults. Yep.

"The rest of Grade 8 was okay. But it was also when the You Know Who guy came in here. I don't want to say his name. He was okay at first; he was a cool guy, but later he became more and more aggressive around us. He said it was fun and stuff, but I could see it was very aggressive, the things he was doing. He started with twisting arms, pinching and wrestling. He put me on the floor and twisted my arm and he would grab some boys by their nuts and say, 'Whistle.' I don't know how that was okay. But he mainly went for the waterpolo boys because he knew them. Some of the boys he was worse with. And the boys would put on a happy face, just because, but I could see it was an act.

"He came for me on rare occasions. Once we were in the swimming pool, playing water rugby, and he bit me on my hand and his teeth sank into my hand and you could see my muscles and the white tendon. It hurt because of the chlorine. He didn't apologise. This was when I was in Grade 9.

"He would just put on a face of innocence every time after that. He would come in at night, because no one would see him. He would close the door, because no one would see him in the room at all – the curtains were closed because it was night. There were no cameras yet. And that was ... urgh. He didn't come to me that often, but he did come to me sometimes. I felt uncomfortable around the room when he started doing sexual stuff to other boys, hearing him do all those sexual things to them.

"When we got told he got arrested I was like, 'Wow! They finally did it.' I was surprised when I got asked to make a statement. I was down at Mrs Bossert's house at the time and I had to tell, which was nerve-wracking because I had to remember every bit of truth about it and I didn't want to think about it at all. Mrs Bossert took me to the Teddy Bear Clinic and that helped. It was a bit scary; they wanted a blood sample from me and I hate injections. They looked for injection marks under my testicles to see if I had been drugged or anything, because I don't remember how I got these scars on my back. My dad remembers that I had them in Grade 8, but I have no memory of how I got them at all. And apparently it's actual scar tissue, not stretch marks or anything, like something hit me there. And I don't remember it, not a bit.

"I was nervous to go to court. I was really nervous. We had to make a few statements after he was arrested because of all the processes and stuff, but by the time we finally went to court, it was a nerve-wracking experience. I didn't have to go into the courtroom itself; we had a separate room, but it was still nerve-wracking because they were still asking you questions and because you knew this could very well determine a person's future for the rest of their life. They asked a lot of questions. A lot.

"After he went to prison, I thought it was over. I thought it wouldn't be mentioned again. I think the only guys who knew I made a statement were the other guys involved. When I heard about the sentence I felt like that seemed way too short at the time, because he'd been doing that for a year and a half technically.

"I decided to stay at Parktown Boys' for matric because there was no point going to another school in matric. I couldn't really move and make new friends, and I had made some friends – not hostel boys, but the day boys – and it was very nice there sometimes, being there and being with them. I couldn't really leave and make new friends … I couldn't do that.

"I want to go to culinary school just because I like cooking. I love it. It's a way to do my own thing, with no one judging me. I like art a lot and I could use that in cooking. I'm very sure I want to do that. I had another option to become a vet, but I'm allergic to dogs.

"Cooking makes me happy, away from everyone's complaints and judgement, and in my own space. I think it could be better with my dad; give it time. I think it could."

*Michael is tall. Very tall. He was as quiet as his son. On the day I met him, he made me coffee and we sat in his townhouse. James was housesitting another unit at the time, so Michael and I spoke alone, watched with disdain and suspicion by a large dark fluffy cat, roughly the size of two normal cats.

"Is it friendly?" I asked cautiously.

"On its own terms," Michael said ruefully.

Michael ran his own small business from home and, since his wife died, it had just been him and James rattling around inside, two lonely men in a lonely house, all three needing a woman's touch.

"It was James who chose Parktown Boys'," says Michael. "His mother, my wife, died when he was 11 and in her last days in hospital, he told her he wanted to go to boarding school, because he wanted to be like dad. Like me. I was once a boarder at a school nearby and I could see the Parktown fields and hear all the sports and the band playing – I had told James about that.

"When it came to choosing a high school for him, I sat in the queue at Fourways High and it rained. Other parents were taking shifts in the queue, but I was all on my own so I just sat there. He just got in; I think they were taking 247, he was number 235. Then I applied to Parktown and if you go in as a boarder it shoots you up the queue, so he was accepted there as well. So I told him it was up to him and he chose Parktown. I think he blames me now, but it was a good school. It still is a good school.

"We went to the Open Day, when you could go into the house and look around. It was very nice. We met the Head of House, who seemed nice at the time, but he turned out to be a wolf in sheep's clothing. From what James has told me, that man should be in jail. We went into the section at the top, which was the Foundation House – it's a heritage home. I wondered why they'd put children in there because I thought, a heritage house? They're going to wreck it. And I think they did, there were holes in the walls and the ceiling.

"James asked if he could come home after the first weekend in the hostel. The boys aren't allowed to go home that weekend, but I went to visit to get his washing. I thought he missed TV and PlayStation and I said, 'No, you have to stay here.'

"But he kept asking. Every Sunday when it came time to take him back he would have a tantrum and say, 'I don't want to go back, I don't like it there,' and I'd say, 'You don't like it there because there's no PlayStation and DStv. Get in the car!' Sometimes I would have to drag him, kicking and screaming to the car, and when I dropped him off he would be bawling his eyes out. And this went on for a year. His marks dropped drastically – and obviously my screaming and shouting didn't help. He failed first term, and in the second term he failed again and I said, 'Obviously, you're not studying because I know you have two hours of prep every day – what are you doing?' Meanwhile, they weren't studying because they were doing push-ups and going through torture. He scraped through Grade 8.

"In Grade 9 I took him to a psychologist and she said she thought he was depressed and needed a psychiatrist. The psychiatrist saw him for two minutes and diagnosed him with classic ADHD and pre-scribed Concerta. I said he doesn't have that – James can watch a *National Geographic* programme on polar bears and six months lat-er repeat the whole programme verbatim. He can definitely focus. He doesn't have ADHD. She was sure it was ADHD. When the court case came, Mariolette Bossert called the psychiatrist to tell her, and then she called me and asked me why I didn't tell her he was de-pressed. Surely that was her job to see? So he shouldn't have been on Concerta and I think it stunted his growth.

"I did notice that when he was in primary school, James would spend every opportunity in the pool and then in Grade 8, all of a sud-den he stopped wanting to be in the pool here at home. He said the Parktown pool was heated and he didn't want to swim in a cold pool. And then halfway through the year, one day he came out the shower and I saw these marks across his back ... Scars. And to this day, he won't swim in public or take his shirt off in public. He says he doesn't know where he got them, but since then I've heard that some of the boys in Grade 8 were held down and beaten with metal poles. But he doesn't remember anything.

"He also told a friend of mine that he doesn't swim because he had a bad experience in a swimming pool and then I found out Collan Rex grabbed him in the pool. And even though Rex is now in jail, James still doesn't go in the pool. So, no more swimming.

"When all this came out, Mrs Bossert took him and some of the other boys to the Teddy Bear Clinic and the psychiatrist there put him on suicide watch. He's been on suicide watch and antidepres-sants ever since. He can't come off them, even now. He sees a psy-chologist every week and a psychiatrist every three months. It costs a fortune, which for now the school is paying, but I don't know for how much longer.

"Collan Rex was arrested on 3 November, just before exams, which I think destroyed all [the boys'] marks for that year. I found out when Mariolette called, and told me Rex had been arrested and that oth-er issues had come up. Before then, I didn't know anything. I'd ask James on the drive home at the end of the week, 'How was your week?' He'd say, 'Fine.' 'What did you do?' 'Stuff.' 'What did you do in Maths this week?' 'Can't remember.' That would be our journey home and then the headphones would go in.

"It's been rough. I don't sleep. Not knowing, I think, is the worst thing. You can only imagine. When the Teddy Bear Clinic sent him for an HIV test, then you start thinking, okay, what did go on? Because there's only one reason they would send him for an HIV test. One day I'll find out. Maybe in a book.

"You have to take it one day at a time. And if I hear something, I process it. A friend of mine was driving James back to school on a Sunday and James pointed to the Foundation House and said that when he was in Grade 8, he had climbed onto that roof, that he was going to jump off and commit suicide. He had obviously never told me, but he opened up to her. I think it was his way of opening up, knowing I was close enough to hear from someone else, not directly – his way of telling me things slowly through someone else.

"When I went to Mariolette I asked, 'Why? If this was happening in Grade 8, and he already wanted to commit suicide because of all the stuff happening at the school, why didn't the school contact me?' So I'm thinking, like, right then and there, we could have sorted out the problems but instead it was 'Man up!' and he was punished. That was Grade 8 and then it got worse and worse and worse.

"James is very naïve. He believes everyone is good; I'm the opposite – I believe you have to prove you're good. So when the bullying started, he got the worst of it, not only from his old pot, but also from other Grade 8s. He got the brunt of everything; he became a target because it took the attention off the other boys in his grade if they were all bullying him together.

"There were a lot of bruises. When I asked about them, he would say, 'Oh, I can't remember,' or 'Oh, I bumped myself,' or 'Oh, I fell off the bed.' It was never, 'Oh, the matric boys beat me.' He did, however, tell me about his old pot hitting him with a cricket bat.

"James has told me nothing else about what happened to him. I hear bits and pieces here and there, mostly from Mariolette, because she was there when he filled out the police report and also the form, where I know he hasn't told everything.

"Court started in August of his Grade 11 year, and we would drive out often to the court, which was on the other side of the world. It was out past Alberton, the Palm Ridge Magistrate's Court in Katlehong. When we were at the court, he was on camera; he was underage, so he didn't have to face Rex – not like Ben – but while I was standing outside, I could hear him screaming because the defence would ask him a question and then the judge asked him a question in a different way and he would say, 'Stop wasting my time – I already answered that!' It was terrible.

"I wasn't allowed in the court – it was a closed court – so I sat there the whole day waiting for him to be called in, round the back, hidden away from the press. Which was a bit weird, because when it came time for lunch break, you all went to the same canteen and Rex was sitting two tables away. I was like, really? What's the point? It doesn't make sense.

"When I saw Collan at lunch, it went through my mind that I knew his excuse for doing what he did was that it happened to him, and I was thinking if everyone did things to others that happened to them, if I did things to others that happened to me, I'd also be in jail.

"I just don't know when it's going to stop. You can't use that excuse. You should know it's wrong. I did feel sorry for him. He was 22 and now he's thrown away his whole life. He had everything going for him; he was waterpolo coach, hostel master, rugby coach. So I thought, what a waste of a life.

"I asked James if he wanted to leave Parktown at the beginning of Grade 11. I said, 'Do you want to leave? Because if you do, tell me now and I will go home and start looking for a new school for you.' But he said no, that he wanted to stay. I think that was because of Mariolette Bossert; she became his pseudo-mother because he hasn't had a mother for years. He felt safe there, especially after Rex left.

"I don't really look for support – I prefer to keep to myself ... well, me and the cat. I just get on with things, keep myself busy ... well, try to. I think I should have done more. I didn't know how, but you can always do more. James seems to be getting better; his appointments seem to help. We don't get on; he's built up a barrier. I think he blames me for sending him there even though it was his choice. I wish I knew more, I wish I could tell you more. I asked James about it over and over, but he wouldn't tell me what happened. He said, 'Stop asking questions, because you're not going to like the answers.' So everything I know I got from other parents and Mariolette. But not from James."

At the time of writing, Parktown Boys' had, with no explanation, stopped payment of James's medication and psychologist bills, and Michael's email queries to the school have remained unanswered. James is still on suicide watch.

Chapter 5
The Boy Who Stood Up
*Ben

"So the beatings and initiations didn't stop after the school camp?"

Ben and his father exchanged glances. The Archivist took off his glasses and started cleaning them.

"Camp is just the beginning."

"And what happens when you get back?"

"Well, for one thing you have to pass the hostel test. And I had to do six hostel tests because I kept failing them," Ben laughed. "They're all on the same basis: you've got to name all your matrics, and you name all their accolades. So you might only have 16 matrics, but between them they could have 20 sports, and the same again for academics – and if you get one thing wrong, it's a fail. You get three warnings, but if you do something stupid, they just say, 'Fail'. On one of the hostel tests I got something wrong about my old pot. And I got shouted at. If you get something wrong or, let's say, if you pronounce it wrong, they hit you, or they just shout at you and make you feel more shit. And they could make you go on your knees sometimes ... I don't know if you've ever kneeled on a broomstick – oh, it's horrible. They just make you feel like shit and hit you sore. Agh, it was more of a scary thing. And then you had to know the history of the hostel: 'So, who was head of hostel in 1964?' You have to know all of them until today ... All the names of the heads of hostels, the names of the buildings, the stairs – you had to know the stairs' names. 'Who died on the AstroTurf? Who was he?' You had to know that the stairs in the hostel were named after the guy who died on the AstroTurf. Agh, you just had to know all this stuff. Just names. The Mali stairs. But you did the test over and over again until you passed, and then you did it in different venues and sometimes you had to do it in front of the whole hostel. So you had to stand up in front of them and you just felt shit scared that those guys were going to laugh at you and swear at you while you're in the hall and say, 'You're so fucking stupid,' with you not knowing what the hell to do. And that's how they toughened you up. You got used to it."

I spoke to Ben about James, and how James had certainly not got used to it. Ben looked rueful.

"I would see him walking around looking lost and I would try to help him. I always tried to help the softer kids. He kept saying he didn't understand and it was wrong."

Ben offered a half-smile.

"In the beginning of Grade 9, I just actually tried to help the Grade 8s the whole time. I didn't spend a lot of time with my own grade. I tried to help them get into shape, because I knew that would help them. James kept saying, 'These guys are teasing me,' and I used to go to the Grade 8s and actually shout at them, 'Are you teasing him?'" Ben shook his head. "He had a really rough year. I said if he needs anything he must talk to me, but I couldn't really do much.

"But by then I had worked out the system. I knew where I wouldn't get into shit. I started to learn what people were like, so I told him, 'Cool, when you see them, do this, then no one can give you shit. Even if you do something wrong later, they'll be lenient on you, because you've done something else for them.' You learn who to stay away from and who to offer to buy food for from the tuckshop."

Ben seemed so matter of fact and confident – a far cry from some of the others, boys like James. Ben half sat and half lay on the couch while we chatted, stroking the family pug. James had, on the other hand, curled into a corner of the sofa, making himself as small as possible, cuddling a small terrier who kept licking him sympathetically. But with Ben I found myself laughing and shooting the breeze, despite the disturbing nature of the content of his stories. After I interviewed James, I drove around the corner and was physically sick under a tree. James's words lay heavy on me. If there had been a time I could have stopped writing this book, it was gone after I spoke to James.

Chapter 6
The Matron
Mariolette Bossert

The first time I met Mariolette Bossert was in the dining hall of the hostel. I didn't recognise her at first. On her Facebook picture she looks happy and energetic and when I met her, she looked so tired, her face pinched. I had heard from a few of the mothers that Mariolette had been a rock for their children when the abuse was first exposed and she continued to be one, even years later.

Mariolette was very nervous; she didn't want to lose her job and said she had been threatened with that before for her constant speaking out. We agreed that she would talk off the record first, and then decide later what to do in the best interests of her family and the hostel and, of course, 'her boys'.

"I promised them I would stay until the last of them finished matric," she said, over coffee and homemade milktart. "And I will, but I don't know how much longer."

She loved the boys, and while we talked, there was a constant stream of them coming in and out of the dining hall. This one needed his medication, that one couldn't find his cricket shirt, someone else had misplaced some sports equipment. She dealt with each one quickly and with care, like a mother. She showed me around the boarding house, the new extension with coffee stations and fruit baskets and some fairly robust lounge furniture. Later she offered to write it all down for me, but reminded me that I would only be allowed to use it if she agreed. Her notes sat in my inbox for a long time.

"I arrived at Parktown Boys' in 2016, with my husband, Chris, who had been employed as the Director of Boarding. I was not employed by the school at the time. When I first walked into the boarding houses, they were in a shocking state. All the mattresses were smelly and torn. Some boys were sleeping on dirty mattresses without fit-ted sheets. There was one dirty old couch for 60 boys to sit on. There was no place where they could even make a cup of coffee. If they were thirsty, they had to drink water from the filthy bathroom taps and some taps were missing. I was not surprised when I saw that the boarding house cleaning budget was R1500 for the year. The ladies only bought Sunlight washing liquid to clean everything in the boarding house. There were rats all over the place. Parents were unaware of these conditions as one of the rules – and a so-called 'tradition' was that no parent was allowed to enter the boarding facility, especially the mothers. The parents could only drop the boys off at the gate. I found it hard to believe that a mother would just leave her child, without seeing in what conditions her son was living.

"The boys had to endure the most terrible rules. Although they were boarding, they were not allowed in the boarding house after school and were only allowed to enter just before dinner time. According to the masters, they had to pack a bag in the morning and go to sports.

"Another harsh rule they had was that if the boys were late for dinner or had the wrong uniform on, they had to sit on the floor outside the boarding house and only got food if there was food left over, after everyone else had eaten. I was simply shocked with the way the masters were running boarding.

"I began driving my husband crazy, urging him to speak to the committee parents when they had their meetings, specifically about the condition of the mattresses. I could not sleep at night, tossing and turning, thinking about how the boys were sleeping on those filthy things.

"When I questioned the masters who stayed in boarding about the shocking conditions, they would tell me that this was 'life' and this made boys 'men'. I was horrified. I knew I had to do something.

"I urged Chris to ask the committee if they would mind if I taught the ladies to clean the boarding properly. I was not employed by the school and not working at that stage. With permission from the parents' committee, I bought sugar soap and we scrubbed everything: the showers, the floors, the walls, the filthy couch, but eventually we had to throw that out as it was totally rotten, infested by insects. I have a lot of pictures detailing how the place used to look. On the first day of school, the teachers had a cocktail party in Surgite, the Old Boys' bar, and my husband invited me to accompany him. The headmaster, Mr Bradley, introduced me to a mom by the name of Michelle Hobkirk; he told me she had done a lot of work for the school and maybe I could assist her in my free time if I was up to it.

"Michelle brought her retired parents to the school. Her mom took measurements and made curtains for all the windows and her dad worked day and night on maintenance, fixing up, painting and gardening, to improve the boarding living conditions.

"Michelle kindly sponsored workers on weekends to do painting, building and help put in cupboards for the boys, as they only had these broken steel trommels, broken and bent, kicked-in steel cupboards for their clothes. The toilet seats were broken and the doors did not have handles. Toilet doors could not close. The showers were totally open and no boy had any privacy. Most of the upgrades were sponsored by the Hobkirk family. One of the parents kindly loaned us R150 000 to buy the boys proper Gold-range mattresses. The day we carried those mattresses into boarding, the boys stood up and clapped so hard and long, it felt like we had just won the World Cup. We gradually paid the money back, after we rented the boarding houses out in the holidays to outside touring groups.

"For nearly a year, I worked full day for boarding with no remuneration. I also looked after the sick boys at night and, in emergency cases, took them to doctors and hospitals. The boys had never had this before. The first night we arrived, we told the boys they could come and see us if they were not feeling well. Soon we had half of the boarding house standing in a row outside our house. We've been told that before we came to Parktown, when the boys were not feeling well, or even bleeding, they were told to go away, or to phone their parents or just lie on their beds. Close to the end of that first year, the parent committee saw the work I had done and so they decided to pay me R5000 per month for working in the boarding house. I was very grateful as we were battling financially.

"When Chris took over the boarding house, we found at least 10 boys who were not officially on the books. When we contacted these parents, all the parents had exactly the same explanation: that a Parktown master would come to their houses or shacks and promise to give their sons full boarding and schooling in exchange for playing rugby and cricket for the school.

"When we discovered this, and the parents were contacted, we found that most of these boys were already in matric or Grade 11, playing first-team rugby. All of them came from very poor homes, most of their parents were waiters or cleaners, unable to afford the fees. The master involved was called in and he promised that there were bursaries coming, but nothing was ever paid in. After these

47

boys finished their school rugby careers, the committee decided to expel them from boarding as no bursaries had come to light. My husband and I were very upset by this – how these boys were used for [their] excellence in sports, but once they were no longer needed, they were forced out, while they were writing their record or final exams.

"When we started at Parktown, Surgite – the Old Boys' bar – was open most week nights. Certain teachers sometimes made the boys buy ice for them at the garage after 9 or 10 pm at night. I only found this out after putting a pass-out system in place, where security would not let the boys out without a written pass from us. One day Chris was at a golf function, so I personally walked up there and told the masters that I would not allow boys to go out as it was dangerous for them to walk by themselves at night and if they wanted ice, they could go buy it themselves. They just laughed at me. From then on they used to send security to buy ice and cigarettes for them. I am sure the parents would not have appreciated it to know their sons had to walk late at night to buy masters ice for their drinks. I also found it shocking that some of the masters had their girlfriends staying overnight with them. Chris immediately stopped this and gave them final warnings. This was when the first real problems started between us and the Old Boy teachers.

"So we cleaned up the bar and only opened it on weekends. It was run professionally and we used the money we raised to sponsor a few boys in boarding, as well as spending R32 000 for the year on the bursary and the sports boys' toiletries. We appointed student masters in boarding to help us with prep duties. These masters did not get paid, but they had to do two hours of prep per week and help us wake up the boys. For this they got free accommodation, food and internet, and they also had to earn money from coaching at the school.

"Collan Rex was an old boy and we did not appoint him. He was appointed by Parktown Boys' teachers Remo Murabito and Dave Hansen, and his position was Pastoral Care. From the outset, I had serious doubts about Collan. I didn't like how he wrestled with the boys and was so familiar with them. We were already interviewing someone else for the assistant master position to replace Rex – having already made up our minds that we were not going to renew Rex's contract – when he was arrested, as he had been given several warnings for touching the boys inappropriately by wrestling or hitting them, and he also neglected the prep. We found him to be very immature and not a role model for the boys.

"The night Rex was caught on camera, a boy, Ben, came to ask me to look on the cameras for the first-team waterpolo caps that had gone missing over the weekend after the boys returned from their game at Affies in Pretoria. We had installed the cameras two months earlier because of a lot of cell phone theft. Ben wanted us to look at it so we could see who took the waterpolo caps out of the common area. It was very time consuming and boring watching all the footage. We told Ben to carry on watching it while Chris sat next to him marking and I was in the kitchen, baking birthday cakes. I had introduced a system whereby each boarder got a birthday cake on his birthday. The next minute Ben made a loud sound. Chris looked up and saw that Rex was in the middle of doing sexual acts with a few of the boys. Chris immediately stopped the footage and came to tell me what he had just seen.

"I told Ben not to talk about this to anyone as Mr B and I had to investigate this in order to take it further. He said to me, 'Mam, everyone knows about this – this is Rex's way.' I asked him to explain why would they let Rex touch them in this way. Did they like it? Ben said no, they did not. He said, 'He does it to everyone and he is strong so they cannot fight him off.' He said that when they went on tour, when they showered, Rex would come into the showers and do sexual acts to them in the shower. I asked him why they had not reported it. He simply repeated that Collan did it to everyone, that it was 'the Rex way' and it was 'the Parktown way'. I asked Ben whether the waterpolo caps were really missing or whether he just wanted us to see the footage, but he insisted, 'No, mam, I was looking for the caps.' I was not convinced because the caps were on the table the entire time. We later discovered that Ben's intention was indeed for us to see the footage and get Collan Rex fired. We decided to act immediately.

"We phoned the headmaster at the time, Mr Bradley, then we called Ben's mom, as well as Mr Greyling and Michelle Hobkirk from the SGB, the School Governing Body. After they viewed the footage, the police were called. After the police viewed the footage, they said, 'Let's arrest this monster.'

"The next day the entire boarding house was called, in their grades, to our house. By then everyone knew Collan had been arrested and they obviously knew what he'd been arrested for, as it seemed like all the boys knew his ways. We told them that if they were one of Collan's victims, they could speak to anyone in boarding. Of the eight boys who came forward, seven opened up to me and one boy to a teacher, Mr Zulu. We immediately informed all the boarding parents of the incident, but Mr Bradley did not want to let the entire school community know at that stage. He said we should just keep it between us and the boarding parents. I was not happy about it, as a lot of the victims told me that Collan did this to day boys as well ... The next day I asked Mr Bradley if the school would help us secure a psychologist to try to help the victim boys.

"The school then got a psychologist, *Janet, the mother of a day boy. Janet started facilitating group sessions with the boys and after the sessions she would come to me and tell me certain details. I was worried about this as I felt she should not be telling me things that the boys had told her in confidence.

"The next day Mr Bradley came to our house with Collan Rex's girlfriend [also a teacher at the school]. She wanted to see the footage ... She had also been Collan Rex's teacher when he was in Grade 9, so she was a few years older than him. Mr Bradley said she needed to see the footage to have closure because she loved this man and she couldn't move on. Chris and I had a huge problem with this request because we felt it was not right to show her the footage. So I asked the Foundation administrator to phone their lawyers to get a legal opinion. We agreed to show her the beginning, before the boys got undressed, where Collan was only rubbing the boy's leg, and trying to kiss the boy. She immediately burst into tears. She shook her head and said, 'This is what he used to do to me.' The administrator arrived and told us we are not allowed to show her the footage and we stopped immediately. She told us she was done with Collan and if I would please phone his family to collect his stuff in boarding. She gave me his uncle's number.

"The next day whilst the boys had a counselling session, they saw this teacher, Collan's ex, standing in the door listening to them. The boys were very upset and very scared that she would tell Collan who the boys were and what they had said. She landed up doing exactly that. She went to visit Rex and she told him who the boys were. She later admitted this to my husband and I and Mr Bradley. She told us it was really hard for her to just walk away as she was feeling sorry for Rex. I was very upset that she had listened to the boys' conversations with the psychologist. I reported this to Mr Bradley again. I told him the boys were terrified. Some of them said they did not want to be taught by her any more.

"The next day, Janet, the psychologist was sitting at our house, waiting to get a room to counsel the boys, when Mr Bradley brought Collan's girlfriend to our house. She was not on a medical aid and Mr Bradley suggested that because the school was paying for the boys' counselling sessions, they should also pay for her as she was also a victim of Rex. Mr Bradley called Chris and me to one side and told us Janet would also be seeing her. I objected, saying that surely this would be a conflict of interest. We stopped it immediately. But whilst Mr Bradley was talking to us, Collan's girlfriend asked Janet what the boys had said Rex had done to them. And Janet started telling her. I was furious. I told Mr Bradley, 'This is not right.' When the girlfriend left I confronted Janet. She admitted to me that she felt she had been put in a corner. She also said she really needed the work and money from the school.

"Janet subsequently gave the boys her cell number and said they could call her any time if they needed her. The boys then started sending her messages like, 'Mam, I can't sleep,' and they would add little emojis. When Janet received a message with a heart emoji one night, she was at Her boyfriend's house and he did not like it at all. The next day she called me to tell me she needed to speak to me urgently. I saw the boys earlier that morning before I met with her and they told me of the extreme foul language Janet was using in their sessions. I was very concerned. Later that morning Janet told me she thought one of the victim boys was in love with her as he was sending her messages late at night with emojis. I then knew something really big was wrong. I asked one of the moms, who was very high up in the medical field, to check Janet's qualifications. Just to find out whether she had ever been taken off the psychologists' roll for unprofessional behaviour, like confidentiality. This was indeed the case.

"Mr Bradley asked myself and Michelle Hobkirk to go with him to the school's lawyers regarding the case and to get advice going forward. When we sat down with the lawyers, they said that we could make this all go away by the end of the day. Michelle and I were both shocked and asked them to explain. They asked us to leave the room because they wanted to speak to Mr Bradley alone. After the meeting I told Mr Bradley we couldn't just 'make this all go away', as some boys had been raped, abused, and that this was serious.

"Mr Bradley agreed. But then he dropped a bombshell and told us that he had just resigned. We told him we were very concerned as only the boarding parents had been notified about the abuse and not the day parents. He said he wanted to keep it as quiet as possible and we needed to put something together going forward. We were building a R27-million boarding house and he did not want this to come out and give the school a bad name. This really angered me and I decided to get advice from my sister-in-law, who was a magistrate in the children's court.

"In the meantime, the victim boys who had come forward were very scared, ashamed and sad, because by then everyone knew who they were. They were embarrassed to face the other boys or go to prep. They would sit and do their homework at my house and cried almost every night. They felt like outsiders, crying till the early hours of the morning. They were teased beyond imagination. They were called 'gay' and 'liars' – not only by their mates and other students, but also by some of the teachers. One of the female teachers told a boy who was sucking his pen, 'Collan taught you well to do oral sex.' They were called snitches, they were accused of messing up the school's name and how they must have liked what Collan did to them, because they did not report it when it happened, how they had asked for it and enjoyed it. These boys were damaged and heartbroken.

"Then an appointment was made for us at the Johannesburg Parent and Child Parenting Centre to meet up with Luke Lamprecht and Rolene Milne, who have done a lot of work with abused children, and for the first time it felt like we could get the boys professional help, which was already late, months after Collan had been arrested. We were told the boys were supposed to have each gotten their own psychologist, right from the start and that it should have been someone who had testified in High Court before. Rolene Milne then started getting the correct psychologist for each boy. Mr Bradley, who had not left the school yet, had a meeting with the parents, where he assured them that the school would pick up the bill for the psychologists and their meds. The boarders would also be taken to their psychologists from boarding. For one and a half years, I drove the victim boys from boarding to and from psychologists, psychiatrists, doctors and hospitals. I had to manage every single boy's appointments and make sure they attended. It finally became too much for me, as more and more boys started coming forward about the abuse. By this stage, 23 boys had opened up.

"I myself started going on meds; it felt like I was having a breakdown of sorts, but I had to be strong for the boys. After all, they were the real victims. Not just of Rex, but of a whole system of intimidation and brutality that was part of the school's tradition and culture.

"This whole ordeal really had an impact on my family life. I now understand why initiation had been taking place for so many years because, before we fixed things up, the boys had nothing to do at night to keep them busy. Just sit in the filthy rat-infested boarding house, where the matrics who were boarders had free range to abuse and initiate these young boys in any way they wanted. It was considered to be great fun for matrics to beat up boys who had to run for their lives, whilst being blindfolded as they were hit with socks, filled with golf balls and potatoes. The younger boys were put in a cupboard or locked in the locker, which was carried down to the showers, the taps were opened and when the locker filled up with water, and the boy felt like he was drowning, that 'made him a man'. Grade 8 boys were sometimes forced to stand naked at prep and then have their private parts compared and made fun of, with boys gathered around, laughing at a boy's penis size. One of the heads of boarding also facilitated a 'turn-around day' – or changeover day – in boarding when the Grade 8s and matric boys swapped for a day: the Grade 8 boys now had all the privileges of a matric and the matrics had to do what the Grade 8s told them to do. [At the end of the day] the head of boarding would then blow a whistle [signalling that changeover day would be over] and the matrics were then allowed to beat the Grade 8 boys. One boy slept in a tree the entire night because he was that scared of getting beaten up by the matrics.

"The Grade 8s sometimes had to stand on their knees while matrics played face tennis by hitting them hard through the face. They had to stand at the stairwell, where matrics would kick them down the stairs. A cupboard door made of solid wood was broken on one of the Grade 8 boy's head. This same boy was made to lie in a ditch of sewerage for an entire night. The boy was peed on by the matrics, while he was sleeping on the top bunk bed. Some Grade 8 boys had to put their old pots' underpants on and were told to give their pots blowjobs or hand jobs before going to school.

"These 'traditions' just kept on going. Because this was once done to boys who were now seniors, it was now their turn to do it to the new pots or 'slaves', which is how the Grade 8 boys were often referred to. The school had an iron-clad code of silence. The boys dared not to speak about it because they would be beaten up. Certain teachers mocked boys who were reporting abuse to us. They were accused of being snitches and were penalised when it came to marking. The worst thing ever is to be a snitch at Parktown Boys' – that would be the end for a boy.

"The Grade 8 camp came up in January 2017, a few months after Collan's arrest. I overheard how the teachers were planning what to take along for their evening braais and how they were looking forward to the big party they were going to have. After hearing a lot of initiation stories, I begged Chris to speak to the two boarding masters who knew our policies against initiation and they promised to look after the boys. I personally phoned the woman who was head of first aid and asked her whether I could give her the boys' Schedule 6 medicine and if she could make sure that they were given it every day. But when the buses left, she told the boys to keep their medicine with them, because they were not staying at the same place as the teachers, who stayed two kilometres away from the boys. The boys would only see them once a day at the dining hall. So on camp, one of the boys gave two of his friends Concerta and, because it makes you stay up the entire night, these boys walked off in the middle of the night to go swim in a dam without any supervision. When the boys returned we had to deal with a number of furious parents. I tried to get answers from two of the teachers who said they had stayed too far from the boys, so they could not distribute the medicine. This was given to us in writing. We reported this to Mr Bradley, who said that the next year they would have to plan better. The boys came back with blisters on their hands from the push-ups they were forced to do; they were hit blue and purple, kicked in their stomachs, and I was told that nearly every boy cried on the camp. There were more than 10 written statements of initiation and abuse. Mr Bradley wanted to take the matrics' prefectships away, but my husband Chris asked him not to do this. Chris reasoned that we must make sure this never happened again and that the teachers should be doing their work and watching the kids, not leaving it all up to the matrics. Why send eight teachers on camp who don't even watch the boys? Mr Bradley called the entire group into his office and said they would have to do better the following year.

"Of course, after all of this I was enemy number one, especially among some of the Old Boys. We were sworn at, made fun of and, on one occasion, I was bumped down stairs in front of a group of people at a function at the boarding house. I reported this incident to the police and took photos of my injuries after rolling down the stairs. Some of the Old Boys thought this was extremely funny, seeing a 50-year-old woman falling down stairs after being pushed by them. Then my dogs were mysteriously poisoned.

"After the Collan Rex tragedy, although the traditions of initiation and abuse carried on, the boys got stronger and began to speak more openly, although it was very hard for them to tell their parents, and up to this day, many have not told their parents everything that happened to them. I became their support. For one year, I sat with boys, cried with them and held their hands, and gave them their meds to help them cope at school.

"When the Collan Rex cased started, Advocate [Arveena] Persad called me in and she said all parents of Rex's rugby teams and waterpolo teams since 2015 needed to be contacted as she wanted to make sure all boys had come forward before the case started. Most of the day parents were unaware of this case, as this meeting happened seven months after the incident, just before Mr Bradley left. It was kept from the day parents for seven months although most of the abuse happened on tours and daily in the swimming pool, where boarders and day boys mixed.

"Luke Lamprecht helped to arrange for Rees Mann to address the school on sexual assault. As the executive director of South African Male Survivors of Sexual Abuse, he was going to talk to the boys to help them understand. One of the prefects suspected that one of the victim boys was talking about him, so he made the boy stand up in front of the whole school. He landed up standing for more than 15 minutes. It was very traumatic for him; he said he felt like the entire school was looking at him. After this incident he began having nightmares relating to the incident. He was subsequently put onto antidepressants. When he had to do his impact statement, he had a total breakdown when this incident came up and we had to stop the interview. Something like this could have a negative impact on this boy for the rest of his life.

"The initiation never stopped and as much as the school tried to blame it on boarding, there was just as much going on at the day school. These traditions were happening in the classrooms, on the school fields and in the prefects' room. When we caught the head of boarding doing the same to the boys, which *Carte Blanche* exposed in 2009, he was expelled from boarding. Despite the school claiming that the brutal rites of passage had stopped, Chris caught a group of matrics red-handed. They had taken Grade 11 boys down to the bottom field. They had to all strip naked and then they got Deep Heat rubbed onto their private parts. The matrics would then stand in a row and the Grade 11s had to bend over and get hit with bats, tennis rackets, sticks, belts and then were forced to jump into the pool. They had to do this for a few rounds. It was believed this made you a man at Parktown Boys'. Once it was over, the Grade 11s could go to the matrics' dorm to have coffee with them – this was called 'the right of way'. But this was going on all the way through when we got here – the exact practice *Carte Blanche* reported on in 2009.

"The parents of the victim boys who are planning a civil case against the school have been accused by various parties attached to the school of 'trying to run the school down'. I believe the school has failed the parents and the boys. There has been no protection for those who have stood up for the truth. Despite me reporting 68 incidents of violence and wrongdoing, no meaningful action was taken on any one of my reports.

"Despite all its problems, I still love the school and I love the boys. But boys have been hurt so badly and something needs to be done. The Collan Rex case was just the beginning. There are at least another five serious criminal cases on the go against certain members at this school. One of them entails an incident at the Grade 8 camp a few years ago, when the boy, who is now in Grade 11, was hurt so badly that he still has scars on his body. There are four other boys who have the same scars on their backs or chests. We've had four suicide attempts. One boy had to write his matric finals from a psychiatric ward. We have eight boys on psychiatric medicines. There are 23 boys from the Rex case, scarred for life. There are also files and files of statements from Old Boys recording abuse at this school.

"This has become such an emotional and personal journey for me. But I will not stop until justice is given to these children. I want the adults involved to acknowledge what they have done to these boys. I especially feel strongly about the secondary victimisation, where the victims have been doubted and told that they are liars, breaking these boys even further. I want these boys to be acknowledged for their bravery and for all the perpetrators to apologise to the victims. Four years down the line, no boy has received an apology."

After Grade 8 learner Enock Mpianzi died tragically in a drowning incident that caught national attention in January 2020, Mariolette called me.

"You can use it. You can use it all," she was crying. "Those poor boys. Those poor little boys."

I wasn't sure whether she was referring to the victim boys then or the Grade 8s now. Either way, the pain was the same.

Chapter 7
The Former Director of Sport
Remo Murabito

The names of three educators cropped up over and over again in my conversations with boys and parents alike. I messaged all three. Only one agreed to sit down and talk on the record. Remo Murabito has been out of education for a couple of years, after being an educator at Parktown Boys' for 24 years. He was in charge of the sports department at Parktown during the time of the Rex case.

"I'd like to have a chat first, and just see what you're looking for," he said cautiously. "I put this stuff behind me a long time ago and I don't want to bring it up again unless there's a good reason. My family suffered a lot at the hands of Parktown and my son is very important to me."

So he and I chatted first. I told him he would be telling his own story in his own words.

"I'm not going to write up my opinion on what you say," I assured him. "I'm going to write it up in your words, and that's how people will read it … I will ask you questions about things I've been told, so you don't feel blindsided, and whatever you say will be what is published."

"Okay," he nodded. "Then let's do it. I think it's time. I really have a lot to let out and let go of."

We met for an interview, I went home and transcribed what we had talked about and sent it back to him.

"Thanks for the opportunity," he said.

"I studied a degree in Education and received a bursary from the then TED, for which I was required to work back. After my teaching practical at a co-educational school, I swore blind I would never teach again, maybe because I battled to manage to teach the girls, having myself attended an all-boys school. But then I got a phone call from the head of Mathematics at Parktown Boys', to say they were looking for a Maths teacher and they offered me the job. I accepted. I went from not wanting to teach to falling for a profession and an institution. In essence, I was at Parktown just short of 24 years. I left in December 2018. Twenty-three of those years were mostly amazing. The last year, 2018, was absolutely horrendous.

"In fact, the last 10 years were difficult, with all the issues the school had to go through, but we'd always risen above the media attacks on us – the persecuting and crucifying of the school and the staff. The school has always been an underdog school and has always punched above its weight. Parktown Boys' has never really had the right to compete on the sports field – they've never had the numbers of their rivals, but then they haven't recruited as aggressively as other schools do.

"During the first 14 years that I taught, we probably had the most dedicated teaching staff of any school – we always went to sporting events en masse and always looked the part. Staff at other schools were constantly amazed at how uniformly the staff were dressed and how cohesive we were. Nothing was too much of an effort and the staff backed each other at all times. We would walk into the workroom or staff room and assist each other with collating exam papers, registers, or any task, for that matter. The staff were great fun socially, whilst being professional in the classroom. Parktown learners were solid and lived and breathed the school. First-team colours were primarily black and there was a saying that was introduced, that "Black is thicker than blood". And that's really how the boys lived their school lives. When my son was four years old, he said that he wanted to attend Parktown and he wanted to board. What four-year-old says that? That is what the school meant to so many of us. My son got his wish, which was sadly ripped away from him by an unfair system, promoted by a handful of people with an agenda and supported by media houses who operate with impunity and disregard for human feelings or concern for printing facts, but rather sensationalism, which helps their rags to sell. I had to take him out of the school, which had been his dream for so long, and put him somewhere else and that just felt so wrong.

"Parktown is almost 100 years old and, like their traditional rival schools, it is filled with history and tradition. To be part of a school like that and be part of a brotherhood, which I believe the school really gave you, was something special. It was not always an easy environment, but no environment is perfect. There's a lot of bravado and it can be tough. Having said that, some of the boys who played first-team rugby were also in the choir or did public speaking or debating and no one ever laughed at them; they weren't judged. The boys were admired and looked up to. As long as you pulled your weight, you would fit in.

"Parktown was the first state school that integrated back in 1992 as a Model-C school, and I think the school gained a massive advantage. It was a time of inspirational leadership by the headmaster back then, Tom Clarke. The boys never saw colour in terms of race. In my opinion, they were distinguished by the blazer.

"I truly believe that monastic or boys' schools cater for 95 per cent of kids. There might be 5 per cent that can't get it and don't want to be part of compulsory school participation, and that kind of environment can be tough for them, so therefore there are other options for them, but the 95 per cent really thrive.

"I always coached sport. I've coached A-team cricket and rugby, as well as athletics. I also coached First XV rugby team from 2001 to 2004, and I became Director of Sport in 2003. I'll be honest, I taught in the classroom because of sport, but I was someone who was effective both on the sports field and in the classroom, where I taught Maths every year.

"Being Director of Sport was the beginning of something special. It was an influential position in the school. Coaching sport is amazing because kids get to express themselves differently on the sports field and it's good for the teachers to see boys excel in an area they are strong in, which may not be academics. I think it meant a lot to the boys to have a teacher coach and support them, and I think it helped the staff who coached sport, to understand the boys better. I believe it helped improve discipline in the classroom. As Sports Director, I also sat on middle management in the school and could try to effect changes which, at times, gave me an opportunity to assist at recruitment into the school. Sports Directors were also involved in the Open Day and indirectly with the facilities' management. You had input on things the school really needed, like when you secured a sponsorship where the money was spent as per the donor's request. For example, in the late 1990s, funds got spent on the AstroTurf and I think at that point we were the second school in the country to have an AstroTurf and definitely the first state school. A further example was also when alumni funds were spent on the construction of the sports centre and then, more recently, with the upgrade of the boarding establishment.

"In terms of recruitment into the school, I would often have to raise funds for disadvantaged learners, whether it was for tuition fees or boarding fees. Some of these arrangements are still in place today to assist. Some of the funds were also donated by my own family members but, understandably, that has now stopped.

"Ten years ago, with the boarding-house initiation and abuse of 2009 [exposed by *Carte Blanche*], things changed. What I understand happened back then was that some sort of 'rite of passage' was uncovered, which the Grade 11 and 12 learners invented. The senior boarding master at the time had heard rumblings that something was planned and he even confronted the boys on the sports field about it. At that meeting with the Grade 12 boys, they even asked him how they would know if what they were doing was right or wrong. He said: 'Imagine your own parents over your one shoulder, and the parents of the boy on the other and ask yourself, what decision do I make?' The boys said, 'Thank you, sir, we understand,' and the senior master thought he had nipped it in the bud. But it went ahead and happened anyway, even though they were warned that such practices were not allowed or condoned. Exactly the same was the case on any subsequent tours, rights of passage or initiation, as certain people refer to it. Physical and verbal abuse has never been condoned at PBHS.

"The school got absolutely crucified by the media and that was a difficult pill to swallow, because a lot of people were very outspoken without knowing the facts. It's a fact that the parents of the Grade 11 boys concerned came to know about the incident from the school, via the senior boarding master. The parents of the Grade 11 and 12 boys were informed that the Grade 12 boys had been suspended with immediate effect, based on what had happened the night before, and that there would be disciplinary hearings to follow. The media never ran that, and it's also a fact that the boys were suspended with immediate effect and the parents were alerted immediately.

"The fallout of the 2009 incident had a powerful negative impact on the next decade. As a result, the school's name was badly tarnished. The media is powerful – people believe what they read. A school's intake, especially the Model-C type, is very important. State only contributes to the salaries of about 40 per cent of the teaching staff and a pittance towards grounds and upkeep, so school fees are very important, and if you're not getting people enrolling then you've got a problem. Sports results are also very important in attracting the right kind of kids, because you're perceived to be a good school if you have good results and you get good results with the right kind of intake, which you need to attract, so the power of positive results is vital. Sporting results make the press on a weekly basis and academics only once a year. I am not saying that this is correct in any way, but rather that this is a reality that is not likely to change anytime soon in this country.

"I don't know how this particular case from 2009 ended, as I believe it was settled out of court, but every time we wanted to encourage boys to consider Parktown as a school and boarding as an option, this matter was often mentioned by prospective parents. It was a case of, 'But what about the initiation?'

"In terms of boarding responsibilities and initiation, all I know is that every boy had a responsibility to keep their area clean, and their bedrooms and lockers etc. They were also to focus on a holistic education and push themselves. Having said that, the duties of the juniors – being Grade 8 learners – included cleaning the rooms of the seniors, their old pots, as well as sweeping and mopping the corridors and bathroom floors. I never heard anything about boys being beaten up by their old pots or sexually molested. That is news to me. The Grade 8s did get their food last in the dining hall; seniors went first.

"The boys at the school generally had respect. I always think I've had a great relationship with the learners I've taught over the years; some of them are mates even today.

"My parents sacrificed a lot to send me to a private school during a dark time in this country when we were segregated. Throughout my schooling, I was oblivious to segregation because I had friends of all races as a kid in the mid-1970s. This was a privilege granted to me by my parents, which I believe has stood me in good stead and why I have never seen colour in my world.

"I loved teaching at Parktown, I loved the boys and my colleagues, and I loved knowing that I played a part in improving someone's life. I'd like to think that 99.9 per cent of the Old Boy population would support me 100 per cent.

"In terms of the boarding-house staffing and rules, you have the head of the boarding house, who is in charge of the disciplinary process for discipline contravention. I was a boarding master and every boarding master had to do one full day of duty. So one of the things we did was in the form of a mentorship programme, and there were staff members – myself being one of them – who would mentor a group of about 10 boys. You'd get a topic every week and the group would spend time on it and you would mentor the topic. On duty days we also needed to make sure the boys were awake on time, rooms passed inspection, that they ate breakfast, took roll call, that they ate lunch and dinner, followed by prep sessions and were there for lights out. If boys failed inspection, they were given maintenance that afternoon, in the form of gardening, cleaning grounds or washing cars.

"We had what were called 'stooges', or student masters, who supervised prep sessions. The teaching masters ran extra lessons with the boys on a weekly basis. I often held group maths sessions with senior boys during afternoons, but also during prep sessions. The boarders were generally weaker academically. It's sad, but I think a lot of the boys came from dysfunctional families, and boarding was an out for them. It was sad to see how some boys were dropped off there at 9 – 10 am on a Sunday morning, instead of between 4 and 6pm in the evening, which was when a master was there to start his duty. There was no one on duty on a Sunday until 4pm, but as we lived there, the masters would often see these boys waiting there from the morning. That's not to say there weren't some wonderful boys and some wonderful families. I believe in the good of a boarding house and that's why I sent my own son there. It was always regarded as a family. Some of those kids didn't have a good family life and this was the only family they had. Some of them enjoyed being there more than being at home.

"The brutality I've been told about was not known to myself, and I doubt by any of the masters. Brutality, physical and verbal abuse of any nature were not condoned. My flatlet was across a parking area almost across from the matric dorms and if their lights were still on after lights out, and there were more boys in the room than were supposed to be, I'd go across and say, 'You don't belong in this room, get out.' Matric boys were allowed to extend their lights-out times on condition that they were studying. If forms of physical, sexual and verbal abuse took place, this had to have happened well after lights out, when masters were asleep. It must have happened in the middle of the night, that's all I can think, because they were under constant supervision throughout the day and after roll call it was lights out by 9.30 pm. Anything that happened after that, if a master was already asleep, then we wouldn't have known.

"To my knowledge, there was no making them standing in their jocks in the quad in the middle of the night. Yes, we did occasionally get them up early as punishment. We would wake them up at 5am and have them stand outside in full school uniform – I mean, there's only so many maintenance detentions you can give out and then something else needs to happen. There were boys who would have to wake up early, at 5am instead of 6am. And then they had to stand in the quad – but in their uniforms, not naked. I never heard about anything other than that.

"In fact, in terms of the boarding masters, I always found them to be diligent and professional. They executed their duties well and in the best interests of the boys. Former boarding master, Dave Hansen, together with a former parent even started the Mufasa programme for the boarders. This was a programme in which Old Boys of the school would meet with boarders on the school campus and mentor them and assist them where possible. The supposed 'code of silence' (besides not existing), which is claimed to have been enforced by the hostel masters, is completely untrue. Why would a programme like the Mufasa programme be started, whereby hostel outsiders – parents and/or Old Boys – are invited in to mentor boys? The boys found a lot of value from the mentors and it was usually beneficial.

"Furthermore, a course of action took place in 2014 when the head boy of hostel was expelled by Dave Hansen and the parent committee for kicking a boy in the face. If the hostel masters were enforcing some bogus 'code of silence', why would it come to the attention of Dave Hansen and, secondly, why would he expel the head boy of hostel for it?

"When I heard about Collan Rex, I was utterly shocked. There have been times when people have asked if I ever had a feeling beforehand. I reckon that whilst I was a boarding master myself and my son was still in primary school, that I must've left my son alone with Collan Rex at least 10 to 15 times, which I obviously would never have done if I hadn't thought he was trustworthy, so it sickens me to think that people might believe otherwise.

"Before that, I thought he was a great guy. I remembered him from school, and I knew his grandparents very well; they were very supportive and he was very close to them. I remember he had difficult family circumstances and they were a huge support for him, especially his grandmother to whom he was very close. He was an amazing kid and became a prefect at the school. When his grandmother died, I actually called the boarding master and asked if I could speak to Collan. I went and told him she had passed away. I said to him, 'If you need anything or ever want to talk, I'll be here.' As I said, I thought he was an amazing guy and when I heard differently, I was absolutely horrified.

"First thing that went through my head when I heard was, 'Did he touch my son?' I spoke to Chris Bossert, the new boarding master, and asked repeatedly if what he had done was that bad – I didn't know, because I hadn't seen the video. And he said yes, it really was that bad. Collan's girlfriend at the time asked me the next day if I was going to go visit him in jail and I said, 'Are you mad?' I said, 'I don't know how I feel about him right now ... I might kill him.' And I've asked my son God knows how many times since then, if anything happened to him. He has always told me, 'No.'

"That whole time period was stressful. We, as educators, were under such pressure. We were walking on eggshells because, as staff, we didn't know what to do. The teaching staff felt the parent body of the parent body of the SGB [School Governing Body] at this point, as well as the one before it, had zero respect for educators' rights or opinions and I will say that the staff felt 'bullied' by them. It is not in my character to be treated this way. I have always spoken my mind and this did not make me that popular amongst the parents on this body.

For a long time, educators have been let down by the system. The Brent Saunders case is a good example. In 2011, four learners at PBHS took the school's golf cart and crashed it into a wall. Saunders, who was deputy headmaster at the time, was fired for that. Somehow, the golf cart was never placed on the school's asset register, which meant that it was not covered by insurance. In order to protect the school's asset, Brent made an irreversible error and lied about the cart being his, so the school wouldn't be out of pocket because it wasn't insured. This was an error that he acknowledged upfront, which was minuted in a disciplinary meeting at the time. People said he stole the money, but the fact is that he replaced the cart and immediately took the keys to the finance office, with the papers of the cart, to be placed on the school's asset register. Brent was subsequently dismissed by the Gauteng Department of Education [GDE], but later he won his appeal case and every subsequent appeal that the GDE dragged him through at their own expense. But two previous parent SGB members thought that they knew more about the law than the judge, who handed down the court ruling in Brent's favour and they refused to have him return to Parktown Boys'. Eventually, a settlement agreement was reached, which was somehow negotiated by the same SGB parents, who had an agenda against certain members of staff. To this day, the matter still isn't resolved. Brent Saunders landed up committing suicide, but the GDE has still not released his pension and he has two daughters. I know people think he killed himself because of the scandals around hostel initiation, but that's an absolute lie. I believe Brent was thrown to the wolves. Over the years I've been passionate about fighting for the rights of educators, but we have zero protection as educators in this country.

"This warning has continuously come true, especially for myself. In my opinion, Parktown management has been weak for years and, during the Collan Rex situation, it really showed. The staff did not know which boys had been molested and which hadn't. Bradley told us that Rex had been arrested, and that there was an investigation going on, but it only came out months later how many boys were supposedly involved. At that meeting we were told he had been arrested because of video footage where he was seen touching a boy inappropriately. We were told we were not allowed to know who the individuals were and if we were concerned, we should go and ask and we might be told. I would rather have known. We could have helped the kids if we had known.

"If I had known that *Adam was a victim, I would have had him removed from my class. I had spoken to his mother at the beginning of the year, indicating that there was a problem and the class was not teachable with him in it and that I needed her support. This was the first time I had taught him, so I didn't know what his previous behaviour had been like. Any kid can behave badly, but usually if you have a problem with the child and then have a talk to the parents, the kid will come back to class and apologise because the parents would make damn sure they did. And that didn't happen here.

"Eventually, I snapped. I was exhausted and, as I walked past his desk, he had stuck his foot out into the walkway. I trod on it, and slapped him on the side of the head. Straight away I knew I shouldn't have done it.

"In my opinion, his mom was at fault because even when I spoke to her, she never told me he was one of Rex's victims and when, weeks afterwards, I eventually took him out of my class and sent him to the disciplinary room, I put the fact on a shared staff WhatsApp group. Chris Bossert – who knew that Adam was a victim – was on that group and I mentioned I had contacted the mom without success and, as things stood, 'Adam can't come back to my class without a meeting with his mom.' There were people on the WhatsApp group who were aware of the situation, but said nothing to me. I honestly believe it was a setup from the get-go. After the incident, I immediately called Kevin Stippel, who had been asked to stand in after Derek

Bradley left, and he informed me that it was going to be bad and I should have known better. I mentioned how Adam continuously undermined my authority and was a disruption in class. I reminded him of the actions I had already taken without success. I messaged Chris to see whether I could have a meeting with him and the mother, and the messages were blue ticked, but he didn't answer. When I later asked him if he had seen my message, he mentioned that Adam's mother had already fetched him and that we would both have our sides of the story and that a hearing would decide.

"As I had previously called the mother from my mobile phone to request assistance, I still had her number, so I called her that evening and she was very pleasant on the phone and said she was driving and would call me back in a few minutes. Later, she messaged to say she was very unhappy and was escalating it.

"Immediately after the incident when I had slapped Adam, he was still smirking and being restless. When I asked if he had anything to say, he said, 'We will see tomorrow.'

"When Kevin Stippel informed me that he was going to report the incident to the Education Department, I mentioned that he should rather hold a full Governing Body hearing as this would be the only manner in which I would receive a fair trial and that I was prepared to accept fault, but that there were extenuating circumstances. I mentioned that if this went to the GDE first, it would not end well for me because I would be unfairly treated, which is exactly what happened.

"There was nowhere to turn to for support. At the beginning of the year, I approached two members of the school management team in writing, saying that I didn't know if I wanted to do this job any more, that I had nothing left to give. I used the words that I 'had no more rabbits in my hat'. Every time there was a problem, I was the one who had to fix it. I told them that, at that point, I absolutely hated what I did, and I had never felt like this before. Everyone was walking on eggshells; everyone was too scared to do anything. We were haemorrhaging staff, and every teacher left behind was picking up the extra workload. I was over teaching for my position and I wasn't coping. We were all in a bad way. Emotionally, the staff needed help. The staff are your most consistent commodity in a school; everyone else comes and goes, yet the staff often get treated the worst. No one ever asked us how we felt or how we were doing.

"The first thing I did after I slapped Adam was own up and accept the consequences. I didn't hide, I knew what I'd done. I still stand by that I was provoked. I had no support and I also think I was set up.

"At this stage I had clashed with the senior boarding staff management over a number of issues, which, together with some unsavoury experiences, resulted in me initially removing my son from the boarding house.

"After this incident, there was another disciplinary matter against Adam for assaulting a younger learner, but this was swept under the carpet by management.

"The GDE had a law firm come in and do an investigation into all the accusations and claims about initiation. They interviewed me, and asked me directly if I supported initiation. I said if you're talking about the dictionary definition, which is 'a rite of passage to mark entry into a group or community,' then, yes, I do. It doesn't have anything to do with physical or verbal abuse.

"Some of the questions they asked were, in my opinion, ridiculous and irrelevant. That evening when I got home, I emailed the school management team and said to them, 'You have a problem in your school. It's clear there is an agenda and there are certain staff being targeted and I believe I am one of them, simply because I would not allow myself to be bullied by certain individuals.'

"Then that other law firm came in – they listened to the audio tape of my interview and they heard what they wanted to hear. I was never interviewed by this firm, yet they made one-sided allegations and accusations, which is why it was referred to as prima facie evidence – so basically hearsay from people who had an agenda.

"The response I got was unhelpful. One of the senior staff members just said, 'Don't let it jeopardise the person that you are,' so again there was very little actual support for me. All this was going on before my incident with Adam and the staff were so uneasy – like I said, walking on eggshells.

"At this point, it must be mentioned that, ultimately, it was my decision to resign. I was never forced to do so, although a handful of parents with an agenda feel vindicated and one family even took a copy of the letter, which the then headmaster, Mr Williams, had sent to the teaching staff, indicating that it was with sadness that I had resigned, and posted it on Facebook, with a defamatory comment. So how did this family get a copy of the letter that was only emailed to the teaching staff? I resigned. I wasn't pushed.

"This exact same parent used foul and abusive language towards me over the phone and when I repeatedly ended the call, he summoned me to a meeting with the acting headmaster at the time.

"I do have many fond memories during the early years spent at the school. There was a kid who sadly passed away, Matthew Martins. I recruited him at 13 years old; he was very good at cricket. His mom had brought him up single-handedly, and he stood out as the most wonderful kid. In Grade 10 he was diagnosed with leukaemia and I helped co-ordinate a shavathon to try to raise money to help the family. So, as teachers, we said that if the school raised a certain amount, some of us would blade shave our heads and a hairdresser came in and blade shaved us. We raised quite a lot to help his mom out. When the story about Adam came out, the picture of me used by the media was when I was shaved and I looked like a total thug. I'm sure they could have found another one (even though the consideration for my rights was ignored as these media houses do in order to sell their rag) but they didn't. But that was why I had a bald head – for the shavathon. This matter was addressed with the press ombudsmen, as well as the fact that my name was published and I was tried by the press. The effect this had on my family, especially my son, was so harsh. The ombudsman could not assist as they have no jurisdiction over independent media houses and any subsequent letter sent by myself and [my] lawyer to the 'independent press ombudsman' was ignored and I was informed that the reporter and paper had acted correctly. It is grossly unfair how the names of criminals are seldom published by the press until the time of trial, but I was publicly tried by the press, with zero regard for the impact it would have on my family and personal life, which still plagues me today.

"I left Parktown Boys' at the end of 2018. When I drove out the gate for the last time, I felt nothing for the school. I still feel extremely let down and hurt. I clearly needed to get out of the system, which fails educators on a daily basis and is one of the reasons why this country is in such a crisis. For a long time, my family and mates who weren't teachers couldn't understand why I put in as much as I did. It was never about the money for me, but when this happened, I felt then that maybe they were right – that maybe I shouldn't have given as much as I did. There are times that I think, well, for what? But then I think about testimonials I have received. I know that I did make a difference. In 2017, I attended one of two annual dinners at the boarding house. On the evening I did attend, one of the rugby boys – whom I had recruited from a disadvantaged background – got up and when he spoke about me, he started crying and I started crying; it was quite messy, but a memory I will never forget. So times like that made it worth it.

"After leaving the school, I felt like I didn't care if it burned down and even now, with this latest incident, with Enock drowning, I actually don't have sympathy for the school. It's tragic about the child, just terrible, but the system is so flawed. And the Department [of Education] doesn't care. I don't think it can ever fully recover. The school itself will always be there, the bricks and mortar, but it's the people who make it. Historically, it always had a good blend of individuals; there were kids whose parents were doctors and professors and others who were domestic workers, and they all got along – they were all one, and that's what made the school so great.

"I'm proud of having made a difference and I know I did. There were times, when I was going through this personal turmoil, that I forgot that. And still today, even when walking through a shopping centre, Old Boys come up to talk to me and it's great seeing them. It has been so special watching learners develop into fine young men, but especially certain learners coming from so little and now earning a living.

"My biggest regret? Having stayed there that long. Sold my soul to an institution is what I did, and I stifled my career path by being loyal. I was never promoted. I was paid more money because I was a doer and a fixer, but I was too risky to have in a higher management position. I speak my mind and I always will and I'm not always politically correct about things that I don't agree with."

Chapter 8
The Boy With the Empty Stomach
*Patrick

I met *Patrick at the Seattle Coffee Shop in Rosebank. On the phone, he had sounded older than his years, and it was only the occasional use of the word "ma'am" that reminded me that school was not that far behind him. He sounded confident and spoke easily.

"I can't help you much with the Collan Rex stuff," he said to me. "He only really wrestled and choked me twice."

Only twice.

"But I can tell you lots about the matrics and the masters. Lots."

"What are you comfortable telling me?" I asked.

"Anything," he said. "I'm past worrying about it now."

Like Ben, he was very self-possessed, perhaps even more so. He knew exactly what he was doing with his life going forward and perhaps it was that certainty that made him appear so confident.

We met the morning after the news broke that a boy from Parktown had gone missing while at the Nyati Bush Camp, where the school's Grade 8 camp was taking place. I couldn't believe it when I woke up that morning to tweets from the MEC that he was on his way to the camp to search for a missing child. The name of the boy had not yet been released and there were many tweets in response to his, parents whose children were there, begging for the name of the lost boy. A lot of people hadn't slept a wink that endless night.

Patrick was angry and upset.

"I can't say I am surprised, but I am very shocked," he said.

I got him completely.

"That camp ... that school ..." There was a brief pause. "Parktown Boys' was one of two high schools I applied to. I was at a very nice international school for primary school, but I wasn't doing well. I was very sporty and they didn't do a lot of sport; it was very academic there. So in 2012 I went to Parkview Primary. I had to stay back a year to learn Afrikaans, but I didn't mind – it was so much fun there. I wanted to stay in the South African school system, so I applied to Parktown and King Edward VII School for high school and Parktown accepted me.

"I wanted to go to boarding school when I was at the international school, but when it came time to start at Parktown in 2015, I thought, no, I don't want to any more. I told my mom two weeks before school started that I didn't want to board and she kinda forced me to. Well, she didn't actually force me, but she said, 'Please just try it and see how it goes.' I always ask myself, often at night, sometimes even now when I can't sleep, 'Why didn't I ask my mom earlier in that first year to please take me out?' Then I remember that I did ask her, many times: 'Please take me out.' But her perception was that I was having fun. And I think that's because I never opened up as to why I wanted to leave. The head of hostel at the time said to my mom that this was something that happened to every boarder, that they went through a stage when they wanted to leave, but that it was just a phase I was going through. In my opinion, he knew what was happening in the hostel.

"Grade 8 camp ... I remember the push-ups on gravel and how they would wake us up and break us down and call us names, telling us we were shit. At the end of the camp they said that, even though we'd survived and we were now considered Parktonians, we were still dogshit. We were told that we had to understand that there was a hierarchy and stuff like that.

"Camp was brutal. Some boys got hit. We were ordered onto the gravel to do push-ups on our knuckles. We were there from 2.30 am until 5.30 am. The matrics kicked dust in our faces and if you put your knees down to rest, they would put you down and tell you you were useless and you were weak.

"We all got back to the school and boarders weren't allowed to go home for two weeks, so I didn't see my mom when we got back be-cause she couldn't make it. We went straight into hostel and met the matrics, and one of the things they told us on the first day was that someone in the hostel was a paedophile, and then they told me it was my old pot. At the end of the day, they said it was a joke. I didn't laugh at that.

"For the next two days we had to do tests in the hall, English and Maths, to rank us for streaming. After that, every evening I would go back and meet the matrics. The first night they were very chilled and then on the second night, towards the evening, they made us get into our rooms and they chose who they wanted as their new pots. We sat on the floor as they judged us about how we looked and who deserved to have who. For me, they asked who was good at accents and who was not from here and I put my hand up. So I got *Jack. He was nice that evening, and told me what I had to do for him the next day. I had to be at his room by 5 am to pack his bag and mop his floor, put his flops next to his bed and put his towel out and, when he went to shower, I would have to make his bed. Only then was I allowed to leave to go do my own hostel duties. I think my first duty was bathrooms.

"My parents were allowed to come and see us on the first weekend. They came and met the matrics, who were still chilled, and I thought, so far so good. Our parents would give us snacks before they left and then the matrics would take them for themselves and I kind of understood that's just how it was. But things started to change over the following weeks. We got into trouble for a lot of things we didn't know would get us into trouble. Stupid things. Once, before dinner, when we had been doing hostel games, we were all sent back to the hostel to change. A few of us decided to shower and then change – we were sweaty and wanted to be clean. A matric caught us and insulted us and said we were shit. Apparently, we weren't supposed to shower before dinner. He put the cold water on us in the shower and we had to stay there under the cold water until dinner. We were in there for 35 minutes. Then we changed and had to wear all our hostel clothing inside out to show that we had disrespected the rules. So we were outsiders, and we had to wait until everyone else had finished eating. When we finally got in, there was no food. That was hostel life.

"And then there was one night when I went back to my old pot's room to do something for him, and he said, 'Give me snacks!' And I said I didn't have any, so he said, 'Go buy snacks for us.' I said, 'No, it's not allowed.' That night one of the other matrics started choking me; he lifted me against a locker and he swore at me. But I wasn't going to go.

"I started to realise then that these weren't the people I thought they were. I remember the day when my mom and dad came to school for that picnic, and my old pot said to them, 'Don't worry, Patrick will come to our room for popcorn and we'll all watch movies together.' I asked him once whether that was ever going to happen and he laughed and said, 'What movies did you think we were going to watch?' I was in Grade 8, I didn't know. Then he said, 'Porn.'

"The masters knew what was going on. It's a lie to say they didn't. The teachers and the headmaster knew about the bullying because they got emails from parents when stuff happened, but nothing changed. They never came to talk to us boys. I think they might have talked to the prefects and told them to be better with us, but nothing was ever done.

"They knew especially what was happening psychologically to us, because once in Grade 8, me and a friend went to tell one of the head teachers we had gotten into trouble for something with the matrics and that they had punished us quite painfully and he didn't take it up with anyone. He just said he would get the matrics to deal with us. I don't know what made him think that was all right. I ended up thinking maybe he was right, that we shouldn't have told on the matrics, so I accepted that I'd just get a beating and move on ...

"They make you do a hostel test. I failed once, and the second time I got everything right, but they failed me anyway and put me in the showers with only my underwear on, with matrics all around me, throwing insulting names at me for around three hours. The third time I wrote the test, I broke down. I passed, but got a lot of shit doing it. They told me to go into the room next to Foundation House, where they formed a circle around me and everyone said I was shit and they threw things at me. They seriously broke me down. I think I was crying and, before they let me leave, they made me play a game they called 'tennis'. Basically you had to hold air in one cheek and they would slap that cheek and you had to pass the air to the other cheek without releasing air. I released air every time so I got another slap for that as well and they did that about 20 times.

"I was destroyed. I thought of the Grade 8s outside the room, listening and I knew I couldn't say anything to them because if I said anything and they were sympathetic, they would also get punished. That time I called my mom and said, 'Please, please take me out,' but I didn't tell her why. I couldn't. She knew there was something wrong because she and I had always had a very close relationship, but she didn't know what it was. She actually went to the head of hostel at the time, and asked him if there were, or had ever been, any cases of abuse or anything in the hostel, and he told her, no, that it had never happened and it never would. I hated going back to school. I remember one Sunday I fought my parents when they tried to put me in the car. I was holding onto the door and my dad was pushing me in. That feeling when they dropped me off at hostel ... I knew I had another week to go before going home ... It was so terrible. And when my mom would come to fetch me on a Friday, I'd be, like, I can't believe I made it through another week.

"The sexual stuff continued. One morning I went through to my old pot's room for duties. He woke up and told me I needed to dress him. He had woken up with a morning glory and told me that I needed to dress him, starting with his underwear, but I refused. He could see I wasn't happy. I took him his underwear and he told me to bend over and go on my knees. His friend, who was in the room as well, pushed me from behind. I tried to stay calm. I said, 'Please stop! I am not going to do that.' The friend strangled me very hard and I hyperventilated. Then he took the mop and used it to clean all the dirt out from under his bed and he gave me a choice. He said I could either choose to lick the mop and make out with the mop, or I could take care of his morning glory. I chose the mop ... but I was distraught. Sometimes I had to lick the floor as well or eat polish or do something disgusting and I did those things. But I never did that other thing. And it happened five or six more times.

"After the first time, I went back to my room and called my mom and again I begged her to let me leave, but I didn't tell her why. I don't know why I never opened up at the time. Whether I was embarrassed or fearful, I didn't know at the time. It was a feeling like you're not on this earth any longer, like you're in jail. You know you want to communicate with the outside world, but you also don't want to because you feel so lost. You don't know who you are any more. You just live in this awful routine. And accept it.

"My old pot and his roommate got into the habit of beating me up many times, and then I got lucky. The head of hostel at the time had fired his new pot because he wasn't making his bed well enough. He said he was having auditions for a new pot. I went and I made his bed and got it perfect because I knew it was my only way out. Luckily, he chose me. It caused trouble between him and my old pots, but he was a good guy. I still speak to him now. He saved me.

"Back then I never ate dinner for weeks at a time. It was usually punishment for not going to hostel sports. I trained every day except Thursday, so I couldn't go to hostel sports the rest of the days, but I paid for it. I was so hungry. I was going to training every day, and I had no power and my coach could tell that it was affecting me. I used to get injuries because I was so weak. I spoke to him, but he was someone who was very tough when it came to training and I thought he would just tell me to get my shit together. But he did come to speak to me and asked what was going on because it was affecting my training. He said training is a place where you must empty your thoughts and concentrate. I think he would have understood if I told him that I was starving, but I didn't tell him because I didn't want him to think I was soft. When I told him afterwards, he said I was stronger now for having gotten through it.

"That was it, until I got really hurt. It's very hard to talk about, but I live with it, I guess. One time I was coming to dinner after training and I was told I wasn't allowed to eat. I was standing outside and one of the matric boys put two potatoes in a stocking and tied the stocking so it was heavy and stretchy and told me to face the wall with my legs open and swung it between my legs quite a few times. The pain was terrible; that was the time I realised something was actually broken. That incident has done lasting damage.

"I always played hostel sports on Thursdays to try to make up for not playing the other days, but the matrics would still tackle me and single me out. And then sometimes they would make us lie down in the sewage pipe and say we had to stay there because we were full of shit.

"I had a good prefect who helped me out; he knew what was happening in school and he took me in. He was doing drama and he would speak to me about it because he could see I wasn't okay. That's how I would get away from going to dinner, so I joined the drama group. But the matrics would come and find us and throw abuse at us, saying to this prefect, 'Patrick is sucking you off backstage.'

"I probably could have left boarding if I had told my mom what was really going on but, to be honest, by then I wanted to stay. I was so angry. I wanted to stay on because, I thought, when I get to matric I would do the same to my Grade 8s. I thought, they will deserve it – the same way we were made to think we deserved it. Later, after everything came out, I told my mom this and she said, 'If you do that I will disown you as your mom.' And then in Grade 9 and 10 I went on a whole new journey. I was sad and depressed the whole time about what had happened in Grade 8, but then suddenly everything got much better. My training improved and I was making teams, getting race wins, and something released my mind from all of that hatred. I knew then I would never do that to the Grade 8s. I would never put anyone through what I went through. Also, in Grade 9 the Bosserts came and the hostel got better immediately. I never had to stand outside and wait for dinner again; there was always enough food.

"Collan Rex started as a hostel master when I was in Grade 8. When he was arrested, we were all looking out of the window and watching the lights flash on the cop car. I didn't know the extent then of what he had done. I was shocked about it. Very shocked. I didn't see the footage, but I heard about it.

"I didn't know it was sexual. I just knew he had wrestled all of us, me included. I didn't like him, but I didn't like any of the masters. My mom used to tell me, 'Patrick, a teacher is not a friend, a teacher is someone to teach you.'

"I thought he manipulated younger boys into thinking they were his friends, but he wasn't. He made them think they were cool by smoking with them and stuff and tried to make them like him.

"I eventually told my mom about what had happened to me, after Ben told the Bosserts about Collan Rex. When it came out, she came to me and said, 'Did it happen to you?' And I said, 'No, not with him, but other stuff happened.' I made her promise she wouldn't say anything about it because I didn't need the stress, and she said she wouldn't. But then I started talking with another boy and we both decided we were going to tell what had happened to us. We came out and told about the matrics and then everyone else started talking.

"I think half the people who tell you Parktown is a good school are saying it because they want others to go through what they went through. The Bosserts hostel is a great institution; the rest of the school is shit. It has lost what it used to be. People say it's a good school because of its history, and it's true the history is very fine, but it changes you – you feel so different inside those walls. You don't feel yourself; you lose who you are. There's something in that school that isn't normal. If anyone asked me what school I'd suggest, I wouldn't suggest Parktown Boys' for anybody, especially for a weak little Grade 8 or Grade 9. Grade 11 and 12 are amazing because you're dominant, but Grade 8 and 9 ... it's a long way, hey."

It's a very long way. And time moves very slowly when you are at school.

Chapter 9
Changeover Day
*Ben

There were two things that were beginning to strike me during these conversations. Firstly, that Collan Rex had not acted in isolation; the matrics seemed to be a law unto themselves. The institutionalised brutality – and the casualness with which it was administered – was very difficult to understand. This made me wonder ... Who was actually in charge? Where were the masters while this was going on? From what I could establish, there were at least four masters living in the boarding house, some senior, some junior. Patrick had been adamant that the masters knew what had been going on. This was backed up by several parents, who claimed they had called different housemasters and been told that there was no initiation, that it had been a practice that was stamped out years before.

Not if the stories about changeover day were to be believed. According to the boys, that was an annual tradition.

"Basically, it was some way into the year that it happened," Ben told me, "and we'd be initiated throughout the whole year until we got to that day. And that day the matrics swopped roles with the Grade 8s. And the Grade 8s got to tell the matrics what to do for the day. So we'd get to wear our matric blazer for the morning, spend the whole school day at school as normal, and then come back to hostel and be in charge. I wore my matric blazer and I ordered him to get my food at breakfast. You were allowed to do that, because they're allowed to do that the rest of the time, and they had to get your food and get your juice. But I took on the biggest oke, and told him, 'Start barking around our table and act like a dog,' which was funny at the time. And we all made the matrics do stuff, no real pain or anything, just joking around. But at the end of the day, they blew a whistle after roll call, and then the one master said, 'Unfortunately, every day has to

79

come to an end. After this whistle, it's every man for himself.' Then everybody just went wild and started moering each other."

I could see how that could work out badly for any Grade 8 who had been cocky during the day. Ben had worked that out too.

"Me and my friend actually first climbed up a tree, and then it was like easily about 45 minutes to an hour of constant shit. I jumped in a bush, jumped in trees, but you get spear tackled to the ground by the biggest oke there and you're in Grade 8 and everybody, matric to Grade 9, can come fuck you up. You can fuck up whoever. Sorry ... you can hit anyone, wherever you want. You can fight back, but if you fight back they just hit you."

"And did you know what was coming when you heard it was changeover day in the morning?" I ventured. "Did they tell you what would happen when you changed back?"

"No, not really," said Ben. "And there was such scandal in that whole thing because a lot of the Grade 11s would say, 'Come here, you know what happens at eight o'clock, hey?' I said, 'Ja, of course,' although I didn't. They would say, 'I'll protect you if you pay me.' And they'd start asking for money and people paid them. And you know what? Those people who got paid, those okes walked away. They never did anything. And that wasn't the worst part."

It couldn't get any worse, surely?

The Archivist interjected.

"The master in charge, he actually told them to start diving onto the floor. You had to dive standing up onto a hard floor of just sand and stone."

Ben continued.

"You had to dive. And if you didn't dive properly, he said, 'Dive again.' You had to do all your strokes and you had scratches with stones and then your body was just red and sore. And then you had lots of cuts from people spear tackling you, bruises everywhere. They said the only rule is that you can't hit the face, that's it. And then after a while it was over and you got sent back to your rooms and your dorms. Some of the guys were like, 'Oh, that was so cool,' but most of them were just in pain and pissed off."

"Did you ever get upset?" I asked him. "You seem to have taken it all in your stride."

The Archivist shook his head.

"He came home crying often. And he wouldn't tell us why."

Ben nodded.

"Once it got really bad. I called I called my old pot 'dude', which was

80

obviously very disrespectful. And that night they just picked us all up out of the beds, took us out of our rooms, took us all the way upstairs to the matric bathrooms. We were on our knees and they were putting all their weight on us. And my matric said, 'Okay, today is going to be a shit evening, thanks to one person calling me 'dude'. And then basically everyone started shouting and started hitting each other on the head and spraying cold water, and we were freezing in our underwear. The matrics were walking around and giving us shit and they hit all of us. Then they said, 'Okay, cool, Ben, you fucked everybody up, go to your room.' And they carried on with everybody else. So that's where that started and I got a horrible name."

"What was the worst thing the matrics ever did to you?" I was curious and nervous in equal parts about the answer.

"I guess the worst the matrics ever did to us was probably in the showers. They always came and showered with us. And always started whacking their dicks on us and doing all kinds of shit. But they ..."

"What?"

The Archivist was staring at his son.

"You've never said anything about this."

"I'm sure I have," said Ben.

"No, you haven't and this is important stuff." He looked at me, "Can I get a copy of this?" he asked.

I felt awkward.

"So ... what happened in the showers?" he demanded.

"Well, some of the matrics ran up and down while we were in the shower and they were whacking us on the backs with their dicks."

He looked at his father.

"I'm sure I told you this. I've told you everything."

This was the first time I saw the Archivist unsettled. He had processed so much and this was new and unwelcome information.

"Was that the worst stuff to happen to you with the matrics? Sexually, I mean?" I asked.

"Well, then Rex came," Ben said.

"And how did it get as bad with him as it did? Was it like that from the start?"

"Ja, he was always in the water with us. And we played 'No Rules' a lot. You can punch under water, you can drown, you can ... you can make sure a person doesn't get that ball ... If someone gets the ball and you want that ball, go get that ball. Do whatever it takes to get that ball. And you can literally do whatever the hell you want. Ja ... So it was quite fun, but it was still very rough. But Rex started feeling our bums and squeezing our genitals and stuff, saying, 'It's fine.' Then he'd start sticking his hands in our pants and pulling our pubic hairs and squeezing our balls again and doing his own shit. And you're also drowning, so you can't say anything."

Ben was silent for a while before he continued.

"Basically, from there, he just carried on ... Small things like, obviously, with the change of the Speedo, you have to get in your underwear, you grab a towel, take your swimming costume off, and in the middle of the process he would take your towel away and he would be poking at you in front of everybody. And every time he did anything sexual, it was all a joke ... It was never going to be a serious thing in my head, [but] meanwhile I think it was completely a serious thing in his head. I didn't really think back then, but I thought it was just playing around, because everybody saw him as a kid. The reason why everybody saw him as a kid was because when we were in Grade 8, he had just finished matric. So he was like, 'No, I was here last year, and it was really fun,' and he started acting like your friend and ... agh, that's the way he perceived himself. And he didn't hang with any of the teachers; he would just hang out with all the kids ... He had to, to do what he did."

"So he was one of us, if that makes sense. And this was happening now in the hostel as well. Agh, bite your ear, bite your neck, slap your ass, anything he could. And as soon as he started seeing that everybody was not talking about it any more, he started doing it to them in the hostel as well. Ja. So now everybody was getting slapped on the ass, not only by him, [and] it actually became a trend."

"So now everyone was involved?" I asked.

"Yeah, and I think we were all just trying to get along," Ben said. "And that carried on. He started squeezing your balls in hostel, and then you'd get to whistle. But you couldn't whistle. And he'd squeeze harder and harder and harder until you whistled. And eventually you'd have to fight back. I started hitting his arm out of the way and I think that's where he got the idea of fighting. And because if you're not whistling, you must get another punishment. And then he'd start choking and fighting, play fighting, tap out when you'd feel like you were going to pass out or give up. So he started fighting with people more often, and then you realised that while he was fighting, he could touch – he could do whatever he wanted. He saw straight away that we weren't giving him shit when he was touching us, because we were worried about passing out. That was as simple as it got. And then he started doing more of the sexual stuff naturally because he thought, okay, I don't need to fight any more, but if I can make it look like a play fight, cool."

Ben seemed so calm, reflecting on it now. I tried to imagine him struggling for breath, panicking and then passing out. I knew it had happened. Other boys had told me about it, and how Collan had suddenly got very scared and upset. I asked Ben to tell me about when that happened.

"We were in Durban, on tour, and at one point he was fighting with one of the other guys, and he was hitting him, so I went there and I think I kicked him. He started chasing after me and just ran around for a bit, and then he actually got hold of me and started strangling me with my head pressed up against his genitals, he choked me, using only his legs, until I actually passed out. So that happened, and then he was laughing the whole time and then, when he knew I was passed out, apparently he started getting worried, and then as soon as I woke up he started laughing again. He laughed everything off."

"Was that the tour where everything switched?"

"Ja, it started in the showers. He came to shower in my stall, because there were two shower heads. And I didn't say no simply because I couldn't. So he got into the shower next to me and started slapping my ass and my genitals and just messing around. I started putting shampoo on my head so I couldn't see what was going on. I had to wash everything out and then he started peeing on me. I was so sick and tired of it all, I peed back. And then I went and got changed. As I was getting changed, as soon as he saw I was in my underwear, he picked me up and grabbed me over his shoulders. He still had his towel on. I don't remember thinking anything; I just remember him pounding and pounding at me, dry humping me. I think that's when I knew it was done. No, I knew for a fact then that it was because, ja, it was enough. But it was also what I saw on the other kids' faces. I saw they were not enjoying it. Then I thought, I'm not the only one."

"So, did you all discuss doing something about it?" I asked, intrigued.

"No, we never sat down and talked, and said, 'Guys, we should do something about this.' I know a few times I'd tell my friends at the time that I was going to do something about it. I just said, 'He's going to get caught one day, and I'm going to do it.' I didn't know when, but I had to do it before anything else happened. I said, 'I've just had enough.'"

Enough was enough.

Chapter 10
The Boy Who Watched From the Window
*Robert

It was late afternoon, a week before Christmas, when I sat down with Robert* and his mother, *Jill. The heat lay heavy on the grass, and mosquitos, usually lurkers in the dusky summer nights, were out in full force, so conducting a focused interview was a challenge. It is difficult to concentrate when you keep breaking off in the middle of questions to slap your legs and arms. Jill lit citronella candles to discourage the mozzies and the soothing scent seemed to work.

Jill had pretty blonde hair and a real vitality about her. She reminded me of a bird, alert and quick. She called me into the kitchen before Robert came out of his room.

"He's been sick," she said, "and I think it's stress."

I felt terrible.

"Because of this? I'm so sorry. Please don't make him talk to me."

She shook her head. "I think it's the general stress, but he wants to talk to you. I wouldn't make him do anything he didn't want to."

"Is there anything I should know beforehand?" I asked.

For every interview, I made the same promise: I would not ask for any details of what had physically happened, and I would not send anything to print that the boys or their parents were unhappy about.

"Just that he's very fragile," she said. "He's still not doing great. He had to spend time in Crescent Clinic after it happened. He wanted to kill himself."

He wasn't the only one of the boys. I felt sick too.

"Come outside." She had made a pot of filter coffee. We took our cups to the garden.

"Why did you send him to Parktown?" I asked. They didn't live very far away, but there were a number of schools in the area with very good reputations, both monastic and co-ed.

"He got a scholarship," she said. "There was a scout from Parktown on the side of the field when he was playing rugby in junior school. And he offered Rob a full scholarship. Part of the terms of that was that he had to live in the boarding house."

Robert met us in the garden. He had that sleepy look that all teenage boys get, as though they've just been pulled out of hibernation. He was lean and athletic, as all the boys had been, healthy and sporty. He flopped down into a chair, arranging his limbs so he could pat the dog and still face forward.

"Do you want to talk alone?" Jill asked.

"Only if you two would prefer it?" I didn't want to separate them – I knew she had been his rock. A lot of the boys had refused to allow their parents into the box in court with them, but Jill had been there with Robert throughout his testimony.

They looked at each other and then turned to me.

Together it would be. They were stronger that way.

As usual, everything went back to Grade 8. To that bloody, bloody camp.

Robert spoke first.

"Obviously, coming into Grade 8 was scary, seeing all these big matrics. The first day we got there, our matrics already showed us who was boss. We had our first hostel meeting, basically to show people where they would be stepping out of line and how they'd need to fix it. You could see from the very first night that the matrics were establishing dominance over us. We were told that if we stepped out of line things were going to happen to us, and that we wouldn't like them."

The following day the Grade 8s went off on camp.

"We were nervous, but when we first got there it was all chilled and we offloaded our bags. We did activities and stuff. The first time we got bullied and initiation really took place was when some kid forgot to pick up a piece of litter he had dropped on the floor. We were told to all gather around this plaza and the matrics all started swearing and shouting at us. The deputy head boy took it to a whole new level. He took one group of boys and then he made us go onto the gravel and start doing knuckle push-ups. And they weren't just push-ups – it's holding that position and your shoulders start to burn, which makes it worse, and you obviously want to quit, but if you do they're just going to hurt you. My own matric was actually fine; I dropped to the floor and he came to me and told me what I was doing wrong. I said, 'Sir, it's hurting,' and he said, 'Stay strong – we know it hurts.'

So we did that for probably two to three hours. Our knuckles were bleeding after that. Although it didn't happen to me on camp, a lot of boys got beaten. I got beaten up later, after we got back to the hostel.

"At camp, they used to wake us up at 3 am and were always playing tricks on us. The one time we went jogging around one of the sports grounds at the camp and our group just wanted to get back as fast as possible and be finished, but the matrics wanted all the boys to stay together as a whole group. They didn't tell us that though. They wanted one group to show up as the strongest one and get back first so that they could say, 'Oh, so you're not a brotherhood! Now you're going to do more PT.' That took place on the final day there and obviously we had no energy for it. But we did it. We had to.'

I watched Jill as her son spoke. She was visibly emotional. Before Robert had joined us, she had confessed that she felt enormous guilt over not pushing more to find out what was wrong, and had played it over and over in her mind, how he must have been feeling. Was he scared? Was he confused? They had always been so close and then there was a disconnect, one she had not seen coming.

She took over the telling.

"I remember the weekend after Robert went on camp. I came to school, and there was his friend *Scott sobbing, sitting on the pavement hunched up in a foetal position. Robert was so tired that he didn't know his name. He'd lost half his clothes and his sleeping bag, and he didn't know what had happened to them. These boys came back wrecked, truly and utterly wrecked. The shouting and the physicality and the lack of sleep, it all added up on these newbie kids – it was the whole grade: 130 to 150 boys. That was my take, anyway. Robert refused to talk about it for weeks and weeks afterwards, and we as parents didn't know what had gone on. And here's where I feel like a terrible mother; when Robert couldn't tell me why his academics were so poor, and he had to repeat Grade 8, I blamed it on laziness and I made him go on Grade 8 camp again. We had a new headmaster at that point, Mr Bradley, and he promised the parents there would be no initiation or bullying on this camp. But poor Rob went to the camp again expecting the worst."

Jill was visibly distraught. I said to her what I would say to every parent, "There's no way you could have known. You can't blame yourself for that." But she did, I could see that. And I knew I would have done the same.

"It was my fault. I put him through that trauma of doing Grade 8 again. I said, 'If you're doing it again, you're doing all of Grade 8, not just what you feel like doing.' Hearing the extent of what had happened in that year, a lot of that stuff, I felt terrible. But the sexual abuse we didn't know about until after all the Collan Rex stuff came out and the boys told us."

I wonder what it must be like to carry that kind of burden as a parent, knowing you sent your son back into the jaws of the lion? I prayed I would never find out.

Robert took over from his mom.

"They warned us on Grade 8 camp that if we spoke out we should expect the worst. They literally told us, 'You are not a man if you speak up.' But luckily during the second Grade 8 camp, I'd earned respect from the matrics of the new year so I didn't have to do any of that stuff. And there was a noticeable difference between what we went through in Grade 8 the year before. The matrics weren't giving us the same harsh forms of punishments.

"One thing I've noticed that was interesting: I was speaking to a Parktown boy who was going into matric this year and he said that they wanted to do the same thing to their Grade 8s. He might have forgotten what it was like.

"When you come back from camp, you don't want to speak at all. I think we were still stuck in survival mode. A lot of us came from the same primary schools, so we knew each other, but we weren't close after the camp. And the only time you start feeling close to the other boys in your grade is when the new Grades 8s come in.

"In the boarding house a lot of bad things happened. The matrics liked to make us do stuff. We got assigned our old pot and you had to clean his room. If he didn't like you he would purposefully make so much mess that you didn't have time to go back and clean your own room before inspection and then you'd get into trouble and have to do maintenance, which was a type of punishment. One master made us clean up his house and also pick up his dog poo. Luckily, my old pot was fine; I still talk to him to this day – he's cool. Back then they used to hurt you and stuff, but now it's chilled.

"Oh ... and in the boarding house there used to be punishment if you weren't in bed by the time it was lights out. The head of house used to stay in dorm, and he would make you bend over and smack you with a hockey stick if you weren't in bed, or the other old pots would say, 'Okay, you don't want to sleep? Now you can stand out-side our room,' and you'd stay there until midnight.

"Some of the teachers were real bullies and they would degrade you and tell you how stupid you were. One accounting teacher I had told me I was stupid and I was going to fail. I was very tired every day from standing until midnight or being woken up in the night so that the matrics could punch you and beat you up. That never stopped, even after the camp. We were still made to do knuckle push-ups. I was used as a punching bag. I ended up being distant with everyone and it didn't stop there."

"And teenage boys are often distant at home as well – ask any parent," Jill interjected. "So what is normal teenage behaviour and how would you distinguish between that and a child whose mind was permanently mush from over-tiredness and fear?"

Jill had read my mind.

"There were so many times that I fetched him from school in his first year and he would get in the car on a Friday afternoon, and he was fast asleep before we were halfway home and slept all the way there. And when he wasn't doing sport, all he wanted to do was sleep. After a while, I tackled him and asked him what was going on. Eventually, he told me it was about the matrics waking them up at night, and making them stand outside or forcing them to do push-ups outside in the cold.

"I then wrote to the master who had got him the scholarship. He was living in the boarding house at the time, and I said, 'Boys are being woken up in the night by the prefects; they're not getting the sleep they need.' The year before Rob went to the school, we spoke to the same teacher, who had assured us that there was no bullying and no initiation and this seemed like both. I told him the broken nights were affecting Rob's ability to perform well in the classroom, and for him to keep his rugby scholarship and keep performing at waterpolo, he needed his sleep. I asked the master, 'How do I deal with it and what do I do?' I got a message from him saying that Rob wasn't telling the truth, that there was no initiation. He said, 'I assured you it wasn't and it isn't, and I've dealt with Robert, and the boys will not be woken up at night.' I wasn't satisfied. I said I thought it was a form of bullying and a form of initiation. I was not happy with it. Anyway, when I fetched Rob the following week I asked him how the week was and he said everything was okay now. But, Rob, you explain what happened …"

"In front of the whole hostel," Rob took his cue from his mother, "the master came up to my face and started shouting at me, 'Look at this snitch – he's so weak!' Then no one wanted to talk to me, not only in my grade, no one."

Jill continued: "And then the seniors beat him up to remind him never to talk to his mom again. And from then on he kept telling me everything was fine. Because he couldn't tell me it wasn't; he knew what the consequences would be for him. And that's the environment Collan Rex arrived into."

What is normal in a boarding school? Is it normal to be beaten on a regular basis, to be roughed up and forced into things you would never even think of doing? From everything I was hearing, this was par for the course. It wasn't just Parktown – I had spoken to friends who had attended some of the top schools in the country and talked about this sort of thing with a reluctant pride, a sort of badge of honour. I didn't see any good in it. I thought it was sick. But for Robert, it had become normal. The Parktown Way.

"As much as Collan Rex normalised the things he did, this stuff was already normalised," said Robert. "Also, when Mr and Mrs Bossert got to the hostel, everything became a lot more chilled for us. Obviously the Grade 8s were still getting it rough – a few actually left the school. And obviously being a boarder was a lot harder than being a day boy, because the days boys bullied you and called you gay because you showered together at hostel. I was doing rugby, waterpolo, athletics and hostel sports. Hostel sports were pretty rough. One time the matrics made us play 'Open Gate' where they got to tackle us, and even when we got to tackle them back ... a Grade 8 trying to tackle a first-team rugby player isn't going to work well. To be honest, none of us thought of telling the teachers. There was no one you could tell because it was so normalised. And the teachers I knew were proper mean okes."

I had approached some of the 'mean okes'. Every single one had turned me down for an interview. I got as far as coffee with one, but he was still in the education system and insisted that he didn't want to go back to Parktown, either mentally or emotionally. I didn't badger him – he wasn't going to change his mind. But I wondered what his response had been to parents while he was still at Parktown.

Jill continued.

"Some of the boys did go and talk to the masters about what was going on and one in particular told them that that was nonsense and to go sort it out themselves. The culture at Parktown is that you're going to be beaten up, hit with hockey sticks and have a permanently sore tummy, and that was just for starters. Others had it even worse. One boy tried to commit suicide."

This was not the first time I had heard about an attempted suicide. I knew about James. By the time I finished writing, I would know of three more.

"Did you always want to play waterpolo?" I asked Robert. I knew some of the boys had been passionate about it from the start, and a few had said that Rex was really encouraging of them, which made the sexual stuff very confusing.

Robert shook his head.

"I didn't do waterpolo in the first term. The teacher insisted the rugby scholarship boys did waterpolo for fitness, to stay fit out of season, so that's why I did it in third term. Rex started with me when I came to waterpolo, joking and getting friendly. He was friendlier with guys who had had cousins and brothers there at school with him, so some of them knew him already and he started bothering them first. At that stage it was just wrestling really. It was quite weird to see a hostel master wrestling with a student. At first it was actually quite funny. In fact, at some point he got a joke wrestling award, so that seemed like it was pretty normal. He was chilled with me, never rude or angry. He was a nice guy. The first time it got weird was in the pool. He was wrestling with me but suddenly he choked me, and he then progressed to licking my neck and stuff. I see now that it kept getting weirder, but I didn't really notice until much later because he was doing it to everyone. And then, on one tour we went on, he choked Ben until he passed out and peed on him in the shower. He was more comfortable with me. He didn't even hide the fact that he wanted to have sex with me. I came back late from a waterpolo tour in Durban and was in my room unpacking when he came in. He tried to lift my legs up over his shoulders, and said, 'I didn't fuck you hard enough on tour,' and he started dry humping me. That was the furthest it ever got, besides touching and licking my neck."

When Rex was arrested Robert saw it all from a window in the boarding house.

"My friend and I were the only ones still awake that night. He called me out my bed and told me that Rex was being arrested. So we watched. At first he was just having a smoke outside the police van while the cops went to watch the video and then the cops came back and put him in the back of the van and drove him away. We were so shocked. The next day we were the most popular guys because we were the first to know, and everyone wanted to know what we'd seen. So the day after Collan got arrested, we were all chilling before dinner and Mrs Bossert came up to me and said, 'Rob, is there anything that Collan did to you that you would like to make a statement about?' At first I said no because I didn't think of it like that. She then said that it could be choking or playing or anything like that and so I said, 'Well, yes, then he did.' And I made a statement."

For Jill, it was a confirmation of her worst fears.

"We were already worried, before the arrest, before we knew what Collan had done, because we knew something was really wrong with Rob. For me, Robert had become very quiet and he wasn't sleeping. I couldn't trust everything he was telling me, because he wasn't telling me a lot of stuff. He wasn't his normal self, and his behaviour around the house and with us wasn't normal. There was one time my husband said something to him that upset him and he actually went to the bathroom and lay there in foetal position on the bathroom floor and cried and cried. He said he wanted to be alone, so I left him, but the sobbing continued and later I went back down the passage and he was still sobbing. As a parent, you run all these things through your mind because what could upset him like this? Was it a girl? Was it his marks? His marks were very bad at that point. Were boys at school still bullying him? Eventually, I asked him the question, 'Is someone touching you?' and he said, 'No, no.' So I got him to his bedroom and he stayed there on the bed, still in the foetal position and cried for four hours. Then he was like, 'I'm fine, just leave me, no more questions.' He wouldn't come out, not even to eat dinner with us. So then to get the phone call in November from Mariolette to say, 'Your son is one of the kids involved in the Collan Rex abuse case,' I couldn't believe it. I thought, 'No, it wouldn't happen, he wouldn't let that happen.' And I blame the school because, as parents, we were so well groomed that we didn't have a clue. We had been told over and over, 'There's no bullying and no initiation,' and now there was this? The boys were groomed as well so that everything was so completely normal. It's horrific to think that in their minds all of this was so normal. It's also horrific that much more trauma came later after the abuse was exposed. People's reactions were bad. The boys who came forward really suffered, their marks slacked, academics suffered. They got no support from the teaching staff and, in fact, some of them used it to bully the boys still further."

I had heard about this. Several teachers had joked in the classroom about boys who knew a lot about balls, one had even said to a boy sucking his pen, "I see Rex taught you well." When Rex was arrested, these kids ended up on the receiving end of a new set of monsters.

"It was much harder with the boys now that [others] knew and, being a hostel boy, all that gay stuff got more and more intense," Ben said. "I was in under-16 training for the Rugby first team for the following year and the one coach saw I wasn't training and said, 'Get your ass to training,' and I said, 'No, I've got a psychologist appointment,' and he wrote me off. I thought, I'm never going to the psychologist again because I've got more important things in my life and I don't want to miss stuff, or be talked about like that."

Jill continued. "Teachers called him names in class, crude comments were made. It felt like it followed him everywhere. Even at the new school, as soon as the other kids knew who he was, the comments started. They would tell him, 'Oh, you're gay – you know you liked it.' One of the boys said, 'Oh, we heard you had great ball skills.'

"It was an Old Boy, who had arrived at PBHS as a Grade 8 in 2016, who outed Rob at the new school. I had to call him up and talk to him and say, 'You don't realise what you're doing or saying and this is anything but a joke.' I think afterwards he was more respectful and he came and apologised to me. But then I had to talk to people, teachers and coaches, and let them know. And Rob didn't want people to know. He didn't want it to define him. He wanted people to know him for him, for who he was, before they heard this stuff. We only managed a good four months before people knew."

Jill sighed.

"Rob stayed at Parktown for Grade 9 and it was much safer by then. The Bosserts were really on top of everything – the place was also better managed. But even though it had got better at the hostel, Rob was suicidal towards the end of the second term. He wanted it all to just go away. Teachers were giving the boys a tough time and there were so many sessions with the police, sessions with psychologists, he just wanted it all to go away. I think it was the day after his birthday that he landed up at Akeso Clinic. He wrote his final mid-year exam and then went straight in that afternoon and he was in for three weeks. The medication was hectic and they kept upping it. It trebled while he was in there. And then, of course, there was the court case and that was just horrific."

As she looked back on this time, Jill looked very shaken. I couldn't even imagine what it was like to watch your child being cross-examined about something he had never wanted to talk about in the first place.

"I sat behind Rob in that witness room. The defence attorney did his job – and that's good, because you never wanted there to be grounds for an appeal. These boys can't go through this again. But the experience was terrible. The defence nitpicked words that were different from what the boys had said in their statements. He said, 'You're saying all these terrible things about Rex, but in your statement you worded it differently.' He was trying to catch these boys out and trip them up. Rob wrote his statement 18 months before the trial and, obviously, he couldn't recall every word he used and in what order. I sat there heartbroken as I watched this man interrogate my child and I wasn't allowed to touch Rob, even just touch his shoulder, or reassure him. I had to sit there, watching my child being torn apart."

Rob glanced at his mom sympathetically. "In court it was weird," he said. "It wasn't scary, but I didn't want to make a mistake. I wasn't taking shit from that oke. I know its gonna sound a bit rude, but I kept thinking I am smarter than him because government people aren't that clever. And when he asked me the questions and then queried my answers, I was like, read correctly, I already answered that question. My mate, who testified before me, walked out crying and I was like, 'Whoa, what did this lawyer guy do to you?' I was a bit nervous and I felt really bad for my friend. But when I went in and the lawyer asked me the same questions over and over again, I kept telling him the same thing.

"I actually didn't care that Collan Rex was in the room next to me. When he got convicted I didn't express any emotion. I was over it by then."

Jill smiled a little sadly. I wondered whether Robert was over it. I wondered whether any of them were. Many of the parents certainly weren't. But Jill was also visibly proud of her son.

"Rob is terribly strong. He's had to deal with so much shit, and to be strong through this, that is such a testament to his character. He knew his truth and he spoke it.

"We wanted to take him out at the end of 2016 and put him in another school. But he had gone to counselling and the counsellor advised that the boys should stick together and support each other. But the secondary bullying and intimidation that went on the following year, and the abuse they got from teachers, and even us from other parents who said we were bringing down the name of the school, it was too much. I mean, we met with everyone, the MEC Panyaza Lesufi, the teachers, everyone. And we were seen as these terrible parents trying to bring down the school. We weren't. We wanted to make sure that no kids, including theirs, would go through what our kids went through.

"After the trial, Rob was keen to go back. He had communicated with the new headmaster, Mr Williams, who said he would happily take him back. But when I met him I didn't take to him, and then Mariolette told us there was still initiation going on there. We had a bad feeling about that, so we didn't go back. I was afraid that, if anything happened, it would be swept under the rug. Again. But I know Rob misses it."

"For me," said Robert, "the thing I miss the most is the tradition and how everyone defends their school. The new school is pretty individual; the teams stick together, but they don't have the same school spirit. At Parktown, they actually take pride in their uniform. At the new school, kids come to school with stupid haircuts and there are no repercussions for that in a co-ed school. There's no discipline. I miss it for that.

"Parktown made me feel stronger. I don't like talking about my feelings – it makes me feel weak – and I get very short-tempered, especially with my dad. I don't like to take shit any more, from anyone.

"Obviously, even though I loved it, I knew I had to leave the school. The last day I was there, and the last night at boarding, I was quite emotional, because I was leaving behind all these memories I'd made, but after that I was fine. The new school is good, the rugby is good. But I will always wish I'd got my rugby colours. I wanted that black jersey so much. I'll always miss that."

Chapter 11
The Boy Who Told the Truth
*Ben

Ben never saw himself as a hero. In his mind, he had done what was necessary in order to stop Rex. He couldn't – or wouldn't – see himself in a heroic light. By the time I started talking to him he was 19 years old, but when Rex was arrested, he was only 16. At 16, I was crying over boys and thinking I was fat. Ben was putting a stop to a predatory spree.

"I think it was, like, two weeks after the Durban tour that I saw an opportunity to stop Rex, and it was the time when the waterpolo caps went missing. When it happened, I didn't actually know where the caps originally were. I started speaking to the players, who were meant to be responsible for the caps, and they started saying that they had left them in the hostel. Anyway, we came back from Affies in Pretoria and my dad was there – he was going to pick me up as soon as the bus came. I saw Rex go into the common area. And I remember him taking in the caps then, so as soon I heard that the caps were missing, I just thought, the caps were in there, and I knew in my head he'd done something. I had no proof, and no one had told me that he'd done anything, but wherever he went with the kids, there was going to be something. So, during the week our other coach told us to start looking in the hostel for the caps. I said, okay, cool. I couldn't find anything at first, but then Rex actually called me to help him carry something. And I actually saw the waterpolo caps in his room, so he must have moved them there. But everyone thought they were in the common area, so I thought: Okay, cool, now I've got a way to get in there and get the footage and make the Bosserts watch it. I didn't actually want him to get arrested, but I'm quite happy that he did – although, at the time, that wasn't why I did it. I just wanted to get him out of hostel ... I didn't want him there."

I had visited the common area more than once since the arrest and the cameras are not hidden. They are very visible and one is pointed directly at the couch on which Collan was touching Jonah. I couldn't understand how Collan hadn't noticed it.

Ben laughed when I mentioned this.

"Ja, but he was thick. He didn't think. No one usually looked at the tapes. They only checked the cameras when there was something wrong or missing. You don't go looking on it because you want to catch him doing something wrong. I think that's what was in his head."

"How did you get the other kids to come forward?" I prodded. "The ones who weren't on the tape?"

Although very few feature on the tape, 11 boys had stated that Rex had molested or abused them sexually.

"A lot of them didn't want to and their parents weren't helping. My dad was great. He believed me and he helped me, but it wasn't like that for everyone. And, of course, some of the kids didn't want to believe it. They told their parents that he didn't mean it and it wasn't anything bad. There was some kind of meeting of our parents and us, and I asked the parents to leave and I said to the other guys, 'I know what's happened to me, and I know what's happened to you, and I know what's happened to all of us. And the fact is he wouldn't have gone to jail, the police would not be arresting him if it wasn't wrong. And I know all of you – or at least most of you – are uncomfortable with it, otherwise I wouldn't have done what I did in the first place. Well, fuck … I didn't actually want anyone to know; I would prefer everybody not knowing. But I just told everything … It had to come out.' And then the parents came back and everybody started telling their stories. When I did come out with my story, most of the people involved knew quite quickly that I had been the one who told. But then there were other kids who started to talk. One came up to me quite often and we used to cry and we'd have a good talk here and there. And he used to say he was so scared of the dark; if he turned around he thought Rex was going to be there. And I said, 'You can come talk to me whenever you want.' I still tried to help everyone. I think I was hurting inside, but I never showed anyone because I just kept on fighting to stay that way, not to go back down to everyone else who was feeling pain … If I felt pain I kept it to myself – I didn't want anyone to know. And I think a lot of it came out in other ways. So it didn't come out crying … it just came out in bursts of anger. If I started crying a little, it would quickly turn to anger and I'd end up punching cupboards, punching doors, just punching … After that it was just a bit of time before I started using drugs."

"Did they help?" I asked.

"In the moment," he said.

Later I called Ben on Facebook Messenger. He was now working on an oil rig, somewhere off the coast of Egypt, and we would Facebook call on a regular basis. He had done a series of courses that allowed him to hang precariously off rigs and paint and scrape and fix. He loved it.

I asked him whether he, like Rob, still loved anything about the school.

"In that school there's pride, there's brotherhood, there's all these good things that I found a lot in myself. And I feel it also made me become strong, that I could help, stand tall, help other people. The biggest thing in my life is always to mainly help other people. No one ever looks at the good that school has done. It's got a really strong heritage and I'm glad to have been part of it. But the one thing about Parktown is that, although everything they stand for is one 100 per cent right, they go about it in the wrong way."

Ben was part of all of it. And what he did, would change the course of Parktown Boys' High School forever.

Chapter 12
The Specialist
Luke Lamprecht

Luke Lamprecht is a child development and protection consultant who is regularly called to help in or advise on cases such as that of Collan Rex. I knew him from his work at Fight with Insight at the Children's Memorial Institute in Hillbrow where he coaches inner-city children. He wrote the impact report for the state for the Rex case.

Luke was asked to get involved in the Parktown/Rex case by both the school governing body and the school management team.

"The reason I was referred was that the governing body needed someone who could help them investigate the case, because the lawyers who were initially approached – who were dealing with the insurance claims – said that they could 'make this all go away'. At that point, I said, 'No, that's not going to happen because there are mandatory reporting obligations under Section 54 and we have to follow the process; the outcome we cannot determine, but the process needs to be followed.'

"So I had heard about abuse at Parktown all the way back from about 2009, with a history going back even further, probably to the 1980s. These murmurings came out during the 2009 initiation case. Then I got involved around the time of Rex's arrest in November 2016. In the bail hearing he had been charged with a Schedule 6 offence, which is a very serious charge. It includes murder, premeditated murder and rape, of which Collan was charged with 87 counts.

"So, with a Schedule 6 offence, it changes bail conditions. What usually happens is that normally you're innocent until proven guilty, and the state has to prove exceptional reasons for you not to get bail. But with a Schedule 6 offence, although you are still innocent until proven guilty, because of the grievousness of the case – which are things like child rape, gang rape, murder – you have to prove exceptional circumstances to actually get bail. Now Rex did not know exactly what he was being charged with; he knew he was being charged with a Schedule 6 offence, but he did not know what had led to the charges. So he guessed. In his affidavit to the court, in his bail application, he guessed certain things that might have led him to be arrested. And so he made them lesser schedules so that he would not have to prove exceptional circumstances to get bail. He had to put something to the court, and so in his affidavit he made certain concessions. And those concessions are what he thought he might have been charged with, and so he minimised.

"When it comes to offenders, you usually get three basic psychological defences. You get 'denial effect', where the person who's charged says it simply didn't happen. Rex didn't do that. He made concessions, and these, I think, influenced the admissions that were made in his trial because he had already admitted to things in that previous bail-application court case. Another defence strategy is 'denial of impact', which is basically normalisation. And then the third defence strategy is 'denial of responsibility', which Rex used as his final defence.

"When they cross-questioned me on the report I had prepared for the trial, his lawyer said, 'You didn't interview my client for your report.' I said, 'No, I did not; I was not asked to – I'm a witness for the state.' And they said, 'Well, if you had interviewed him, he would have told you that this is what was taught to him.' At which point I said, 'Well, then tell me who those people are that did those things to him and I will go after them as hard as I have gone after him.' The defence attorney subsequently went back to Collan, but he refused to name any perpetrator.

"I've heard a theory going around that the people who were implicated in some way got to him and silenced him, because he appeared to be willing to talk, and then suddenly he decided not to. He had no actual evidence in mitigation of sentence. I mean, he just said it was done to him. But he never presented evidence to this claim; he just simply made these assertions.

"When he pleaded not guilty with admissions, he must have understood it would be taken as a guilty plea. I think two things happened here. The first was the admissions he had already made, so he couldn't now go back on those in terms of the bail application. You can't go back on something you've said in a different court case, because then you're obviously not reliable. And the second thing is the video. There was actual hard physical evidence, so he could not dispute the charge because there's video evidence of it. However, a guilty plea is not the same as what he did. Because if you plead guilty, you plead guilty to the wrongfulness of what you did, the consequences, the understanding of all of that, but instead he tried to use 'denial of impact' and said, 'Yes, this happened, but it wasn't bad because this is what they taught me.' This is not a real guilty plea. It's denial of responsibility and denial of impact. So he tried to do both, saying, 'This happened but it was taught to me and it wasn't that bad.'

"The South African Sexual Offences Act is really clear. You've got three kinds of offences: a non-contact offence (like pornography), then you've got a contact offence without penetration or violation, and then you've got rape, which is with penetration. During my research, I came across a blog post on a Parktown Boys website where a newspaper article mentioned that oral sex was used in initiation back in 2009. Two educators were implicated and a whole range of boys. I think what happened with those boys was that there was a settlement, obviously by the school or whoever settled it. But it was only for the physical assaults. They never ever went down the sexual route.

"When I looked at it I said, 'But hang on, looking at this system in 2009, there's an article that says oral sex was used as a form of initiation. Where's the sexual offence? Who was charged with a sexual offence? Absolutely nobody. Adding to that, the charges against the adults fell away – I have no idea how. A non-disclosure agreement was signed and then that was used later with the Rex case, to say, no, we can't talk to you because we've signed a non-disclosure ... Now that was just simply not true. This was a serious Schedule 6 state case.

"Parktown Boys' isn't the only school I've looked into. Look, I've been into other boys' hostels where sexual things have happened as part of initiation. So sexual offences weren't front of mind. They became front of mind when I started researching and trying to find out more because my brief was to uncover the code of silence. I had to go back in time to work out how the code of silence worked.

"Along with this code of silence, there were other very interesting things about the Parktown Boys' school culture. One thing was that it was run very much like a military order, a lot like a war memorial. On Remembrance Day, the school has a ceremony to honour the Parktown boys who served and fell in World War II. And every time you walk past the war dead, you've got to honour them, you've got to keep the lineage, the lineage is red, the lineage is blood, it's pain and sacrifice, it's all those things.

"Now that whole military-establishment concept is about a bonding through trauma. And, along with this military thing, there was definitely confusion around homophobia. There was a really interesting kind of dynamic because people didn't know what to do with this stuff. From the MEC to his spokesperson, everyone was, like, what do you do with this? It was just bizarre. It's not that they were caught off guard – they just didn't know how to reconcile all these tough boys with their own homophobia and the grievousness of the crime. And then when those 327 charges came out, it was, like, 'Just what the hell is going on here?' So I realised that there had never been a conversation about this before and so there was not a language [in which] to have this discussion. What eventually emerged was that they simply didn't know what to do. So I went in … I went in with Rees Mann from South African Male Survivors of Sexual Abuse to create a language for it. That was one of the big things to tackle.

"The first thing that has to happen is a dispelling of myths around surviving sexual abuse. When men are abused, some of the myths are as follows: 'He chose me because I must have given off a vibe that I was gay.' So there's the homophobia, and that's a massive part of it. Next one is, 'I am a real man, not a man being real.' This concept of 'real men' I challenged in a big way. I just wanted them to be real; I'm not fucking interested in being a real man, I don't know what a real man is. It's a ludicrous concept.

"Now, what happens in a military establishment is that it's all about the code of silence, of boys not speaking out. These are the spoils of war. There's a lot of male rape in war, by the way, which people don't talk about. And then obviously there was definitely a culture of secrecy at the school, but please remember that there are two cultures of secrecy. One of them involves the culture of secrecy around sexual abuse and men experimenting and having sex with other men.

"But the overarching secrecy is the secret society thing, which gives you access to some form of privilege. And in that society, if you endure, you will be rewarded. It's called trauma bonding. What happens is that you are bonded in trauma. You often see a lot of white men of my age (50-something) standing around a braai, and they don't know what to really talk about. So they are all cheering and drinking and slapping each other's backs and talking about what they want to do to that 'thing' (girl) of 20 – often the age of their own children – but you can't talk about their wives or children like that.

These are damaged men, but they will say, 'Oh, we turned out fine.' But my thing is: Are they really fine? Because I don't think they are so much.

"I think most of these men are deprived of an emotional and sexuality vocabulary, and so what happens is that we rape and plunder and pillage when we go out and we drink and score the chicks and bang this one or that one. And that was big at Parktown Boys'. That happened in Surgite House, where strippers were brought to the school, where teachers got drunk. I call this a deviant sexuality, because I do believe it's deviant, and this was massive. So you've got to score with a woman, because you can't possibly say you might have had a man touch you because then you will be, like, a moffie or something.

"The other thing is that when men are abused, they are usually asked, why didn't you fight back? And then sort of the final leg of it is that – and this was used by Collan in his defence – men who are abused become abusers. Therefore, you're not a real man, you are gay, you did not fight back, you do not cry because cowboys don't cry and, oh, by the way, you're also a paedophile. So now we won't let you near any children.

"So the disincentives for disclosure by men are enormous and the only way to reverse that is to dispel the myths and create a new language by which they can narrate a new and real conversation, to find words that they might be thinking in their heads, to give voice to what it is that they're thinking. And that really is done through therapy. So you do a mass awareness intervention, and then you land the concepts and then people who are more experienced are needed to help individuals who need time to work through these things. Much like the mother bird taking a worm and giving it back to the baby bird, in digestible pieces. Because you're not going to stand up in that crowd and say, 'By the way, it was me – I was abused.' What you're going to do is try to go quietly and that causes what's called 'splitting'. Now splitting is a very dangerous – you see it a lot in divorces ... Basically, splitting is something that's all good or all bad. It's black or white, not fifty shades of grey. It's either, 'I'm a real man and a Parktonian. Or I'm not. This is the Parktown way, so if I don't follow it, then I'm not a real man.' And because so much of male identity – especially for the boys in the hostel, which is a total institution – is governed by that system; it holds absolute power.

"It's not just Parktown – this is in general – but Parktown is a specific example of where this happened. When our law talks about the fact that somebody is innocent until proven guilty, what we must never forget is that it assumes that the victim is lying until you can prove the opposite beyond a reasonable doubt. So the perpetrator is innocent until proven guilty. Fair enough. But what message does that send to the victim? The message is: you have to now convince us. While an accused has to prove nothing at all until they're sentenced. They're just there to cast doubt on the witnesses. And what then happens is that they say, okay, well now there's no proof. And this is where it went wrong, initially... In 2009, there was no proof. I said, listen to me: number one, you don't need proof to make a report. The reason you're reporting a case is to find proof. It's not your job, it's the police's job. If they don't find proof there won't be a case. Because most people involved in 2016 were saying there was no proof.

"In fairness, many of the people I dealt with were kind: Kevin Stippel; the acting headmaster, was very good; Mr Greyling on the SGB ... they were both kind men. They tried at all times to play fair and neutral. Whereas a lot of the others – and I'm talking about a long list of names, of teachers and masters alike, men and women, all of those people – were basically saying, 'There's no proof.'

"It was a mess when I got there. And what people must understand about Section 54 is that my job was to believe who told me, meaning a child, because 54 refers to children and people with mental disability. My job was to just report what they said to me. Anyway, there was panic that people were going to get sued if they spoke. 'No, you're not,' I said. 'You're not going to get sued if you act in good faith and in accordance with the legislation.' And if anybody is going to be sued for lying, it will be the person who lied. But you can't change the events when you start reporting them, because that's where everything falls apart. So basically what I said to them is that, very simply, 'I don't care what you say, number one, or what your lawyers say. I'm telling you what it is. And what it is is that we *report*. The police investigation, it's their job to find proof; it's your job to hand them what you have; it's your job to make statements, to tell the truth, the whole truth and nothing but the truth, so help you God, which means, don't lie. Don't lie about things. And the law will take its course.' That took a lot of getting used to for a lot of people, because nothing like this had ever been dealt with before.

"We weren't there to press charges. The state and the prosecutor do that. What we had to do was take what we were being told and then request an investigation by the police into the circumstances that gave rise to the incident – in this case, sexual assault.

"What I was there as was a witness. As a witness for the state. My task was to stand up and tell the court what happened to the victims, otherwise there was no case. And that's what's very hard about the criminal justice system. That in order to prove what they're trying to prove, they have to get evidence, because all evidence is led viva voce [orally, rather than in writing] in our country and children have to testify under certain conditions and all of that, but they have to testify. So that terrifies people. This is another disincentive. You've got to go through the court process. The court process is terrible. They're going to rip you to pieces, they're going to bring up your sexual history ... So, at PBHS, there was all of this disincentive to disclose.

"There were accusations made by some people that the boys had been coached. In fact, a group of educators said that the boys were coached because there was a fight for the hostel territory. What was interesting is how the lines then got drawn. So you have the Department, which, I must say in fairness to them, did what was procedural. They did their job, whatever that was, but they did it. And then you had the SGB very divided. Then you had the school management team in a very difficult position, and I must say that the acting headmaster, Kevin Stippel, with all respect to him, managed it as well as he could have. In hindsight, he couldn't have done things differently; I think, he was completely trapped. He tried his best.

"So the splitting that was happening amongst the adults also started happening amongst the children. Then there were all of these kind of snide comments; the homophobia came up and then there were negative messages being sent about the kids ... All of that causes what is called 'secondary trauma'. So you've got the primary trauma of the alleged abuse – and remember that the boys in the hostel were completely traumatised already. The basic anatomy of trauma is that, when you are traumatised, your primal brain kicks in, and you either go into the sympathetic system fight-or-flight, or you go parasympathetic which is freeze-and-block, and then you pass out. But, either way, what does happen is that you have a massive dump of a whole lot of chemicals. And the first chemical is adrenaline, which is the fight-or-flight. So imagine now that the institution that totally controls you, like school, is the place where you're supposed to be kept safe, but it's also the place that traumatises you. So the impact of the trauma is massive. It's higher than if you were abused, say, by an uncle and you went home to tell your mom and your mom believed you. Here, at boarding school, there was no place to return to safety. Plus, it was an accidental, not a purposeful disclosure. Now that tells you a whole other story. Because purposeful disclosure is: if I tell, I've thought through all the consequences and I believe I will get a response. Whereas, in this case, there was an accidental disclosure: Rex was caught on the cameras. And what this does is cause tremendous stress in the victims, because it happens before they are ready to disclose and it's not even a foregone conclusion that they ever would have. That's where the secondary trauma comes from. Some of them never would have disclosed. Remember the code of silence, the Parktown way ... And although one would hope that eventually there would be a space in which they could, as things stood, no one was going to be reporting anything. Except for Ben.

"So that's why the idea of accidental disclosure is important, because what we must remember is that Collan didn't tell anyone he was doing this. So when he says, 'Oh, by the way, you know, it was nothing wrong – we were doing whatever games we were doing; this is what we did in waterpolo,' he wasn't telling a lie. The power lies in the secret and when you've got an institution that builds on secrecy that gives you access to privilege, you allow this to happen. You don't make it happen, you don't cause it, you don't encourage it, but you create an environment in which it occurs and flourishes. And the secondary trauma was caused primarily by the talk, which is very immature talk, and very damaging: that these boys must have been moffies, how Collan was such a great guy and he couldn't possibly have done this because he was a teacher ... And the immaturity of it came about because they didn't have a language for it. I mean, even adults didn't have a language for it. So that whole cascade of things caused those boys enormous anguish. And it's absolutely tragic, frankly."

Chapter 13
The Boy Who Loved his School
*Seth

I met *Angela a long time before I had any contact with her son *Seth. At first, she wasn't sure he would want to talk to me and I had to make it clear when speaking to all parents that I would not approach their sons without talking to them first and that, if the boys didn't want to talk, I would not approach them directly. I wanted to get a picture of what they had been through, not put them through any further pain. And Angela had been right – Seth hadn't been too keen at first, so I was surprised when, in January 2020, I received a message from his mother saying that Seth wanted to talk to me.

"Do you know why?" I asked.

"I'm not sure, but I think the incident with the young boy who drowned has really affected him."

Angela herself had spoken to me towards the end of 2019. She had still been very emotional about what had happened. We sat in a closed office so her colleagues wouldn't see her cry.

"I clearly remember when it happened. It was November 2016 and my son, Seth, was in Grade 9. My ex-husband, Seth's father, who was overseas at the time, got the email to say someone in the hostel had been arrested for molesting the boys. Seth's dad called me and asked, 'What's happening?' and I called Seth and said, 'There's a hostel master arrested for sexually abusing the boys,' and he said straight away, 'Is it Rex?' I asked him why he'd mentioned Collan Rex straight up, and he was like, 'No, just because he rough houses with us and gets rough with us.' There and then, I asked him if anything had happened to him, and he said, 'No, no, no.'

"Seth had to go into boarding school, as it was really too far for me to drive in the mornings. But he was very soft and sensitive and I think his father thought going to Parktown would be good for him and would maybe harden him up a bit. I think that is Seth's father's biggest regret, because Rex was there to meet them at the gate and I don't think he has ever forgiven himself for basically handing his son over to a paedophile.

"My ex wouldn't do the court case or anything. Even when the last bit of the judgment and sentencing was happening, he didn't want to know about it. We kept a lot of stuff back from him because he didn't want to know, and we didn't want it to affect his relationship with Seth.

"When the case went further and Rex was charged, Seth still told me he didn't think anything was bad. But he did tell me that they would play-wrestle and sometimes his pants would come undone and Rex's hand would go there, but he thought it was like an accident and not anything wrong.

"When I found out Seth was one of the 23 boys testifying, then I knew something really bad had happened. But he still wouldn't tell me everything. He wrote the statement for the police and I asked for a copy, but I never got it. Seth didn't want to talk about it and I thought that was very strange because he and I were so close. His father left when he was very young, so it was always just him and me, we were like the two musketeers through everything; we were as close as a mom and son could be.

"The worst day was when Rex admitted he had sexually abused Seth so Seth couldn't testify to that, because Rex had already admitted to it. I think, in a clever way, his lawyer said, 'If you don't want all these boys to testify against you, admit guilt to the ones you hurt the worst, because if you admit guilt now, then they can't testify against you in open court for the sexual abuse.' And that day Mariolette Bossert phoned me and said Rex had admitted he had sexually molested 12 of the boys and 'your son is one of them' – that broke me. It really, really broke me because then I knew things were a lot worse than I had thought they were.

"My mind was everywhere. All I could think was that he had hurt my baby and that, through all of it, Seth was trying to be so strong. I found out that when he was talking to the police he said, 'I didn't tell my mom because she'd been through so much and I didn't want her to go through the hurt I was going through.' And that broke my heart more because I wanted to be there to go through the hurt with him. But he was trying to protect me, so that's why he never said anything.

"Initially, Seth really didn't want to make a statement. I don't think he really understood the severity of what had happened, but when they got people in to talk to the boys and explain why it was wrong, then he became one of the 23. But he still didn't tell me everything. He wrote his statement with the police. No one even told me that was happening and I was very angry when I found out about it. Shouldn't someone have called to tell me, at least to get my permission or let me know so I could be there with him? The school said, 'Well, it's legal if the child gives his permission,' and I said, 'He's 15 and I'm his mother! Shouldn't he speak to me about that first?' Look, I couldn't force him to open up or relive it or tell me about it.

"Grade 8 is supposed to be a good experience, not like that.

"Seth was a very happy, talkative, social boy before all this happened, but then he became very introverted and withdrawn and stopped talking to me. I became nervous, especially as it got closer towards the court case. I think at the beginning of the process he wanted to be brave, and then a week before, he decided he didn't want to testify. And I said, 'You can't pull out now.' So he braved it.

"I went to court on as many of the days as I could get time off work for, but Seth still didn't talk too much about it.

"The night before my son had to testify, it was scary because I was so worried he was going to do something to himself. In fact, I heard a noise in the bathroom that night and I ran downstairs because I thought Seth might have hurt himself. He really didn't want to testify – he was so scared. He didn't know what he was going to be asked, what he would have to relive. They did it in camera so he wasn't in the courtroom itself. When we went through to court, that was the first time I saw Rex again and it was weird because when I saw him during the Grade 8 year he seemed like such a small guy, almost a child himself, but when I saw him in court he seemed really big and I don't know if it was because he had hurt my child that he seemed so much bigger.

"On the day, Seth was one of five boys who had to testify. The judge stopped it after Seth and said he had heard enough; he didn't want to hear any more. I thought that was very unfair to all of them, especially as all of them had prepared.

"The judge wouldn't let me into the court when Seth was testifying, but I listened at the door. I heard him say how Rex threw him against walls and punched him and threw him down on the ground, and then they asked if there was anything he wasn't telling them, and he said, 'Besides the other sexual stuff?' So then I knew that had happened. Rex's lawyer said, 'Well, why didn't you tell anyone that this was happening to you?' And I heard him say, 'Because I was in Grade 8 and I saw Rex sexually abusing and wrestling all the boys around me, so I thought this is what high school was about.' And again that, as a mother, broke my heart; that he thought this was what high school was about, that you go to school and this is what happens to you. He was so young – he was only 13 years old.

"Until the judgment, I didn't think the judge was on our boys' side. When he refused to see the video of Rex actually choking one of the boys, I started going mad in the court and was asked to leave the courtroom. And then, when the judge gave his sentence – 23 years! – I thought it was so harsh, but when I told Seth what Rex had got, he said, 'That's not long enough.' I said, 'Boy, that's nearly life.' That also broke me because I thought, if Seth didn't think that his sentence was long enough, that showed me that Rex had hurt him a lot more and should have been punished a lot longer. It's difficult to talk to him about it now that Rex is gone away, because he wants to move on.

"My new husband is very supportive of both me and Seth. And my work was really understanding; when I had to take time off work to go to court, my boss always said, 'No, you must go. You mustn't worry.'

"Seth liked the psychologist he went to see and he liked that he didn't have to tell her about what happened with Rex; he could talk about other stuff, like girlfriends and school generally. Mariolette and Chris were always there to support us. I know Mariolette took a lot of flak from the school for how hard she fought for our boys, and she was so good to them. They even took Seth away with them to go camping. We got very little support from the rest of the school. I called often to try to find out what was going on with the boys and the case, but I got very little joy. The headmaster at the time got out very quickly after all this happened. Luckily, Mariolette was great and she kept me up to date with everything. And Mr Williams, the new headmaster, of course he was also good. He was always telling Seth that he had his support and the school was behind him, so I thought that was good. It really made a difference to us.

"Before Mr Williams came to be headmaster, I felt like the acting headmaster, Kevin Stippel, didn't know how to talk to the parents. I felt sorry for him, because he was left with all of it and he didn't know how to deal with it, but he had to. I remember when Seth went to testify, Mr Williams called him to wish him luck and tell him they were all there for him. He organised that the other boys wore blue ribbons to support the ones who were testifying in court. On one hand, this was a good thing, but on the other, I think the boys involved would have liked to forget it.

"Seth wanted to be a doctor when he was younger, but now he's not sure. His marks aren't what they were. In Grade 7 his Maths marks were some of the top in the country at Maths Olympiad level, but he's not achieving that now; the whole Rex thing has definitely affected his studies. He gets 50s now.

"I think a lot of the moms felt guilty. I felt guilty. I mean, how could I not have known? When we took him there for Grade 8 I was devastated – my baby was leaving the nest for boarding school and how was I going to live without him at home with me? The receptionist asked me why I didn't want him to go to the school, and I said I wanted him to go closer to home. And then she said, 'Oh, that incident happened 12 years ago and none of the teachers here were even there then.' And I didn't even know what she was talking about and I had to go Google it to find out about the 2009 initiation scandal. Then I was very worried about anything from an initiation point of view, but Seth always told me not to worry, that they only had to do silly things like have a rock for a girlfriend or wear a big placard with something silly written on it.

"If I have to think of Collan Rex now … it's a very difficult thing. In the beginning when it first came out, I did feel sorry for him because he was young, and although it was horrible because it happened to my son and he hurt my son badly, I thought maybe he hadn't understood what he was doing, and maybe it was the fact that it was done to him, and maybe it would have been different if he was a 40-year-old man or teacher. He was so young at the time and it was done to him when he was in school. From that aspect, I felt sorry for him and when he got those 23 years, I thought, 'Wow, that's a long time. But on the flip side of the coin, for my son – and, remember, I don't know everything that happened to him – for him to think it wasn't harsh enough … I was very torn. Seeing Rex at court made me less sorry for him because he was so arrogant. He was smiling at everyone and he didn't seem remorseful at all."

I only met with Seth weeks later. As I had committed to all the parents, I promised not to badger them, or to approach their sons except through them. I also said I wouldn't push. Angela didn't think Seth would want to talk to me, and after I spoke to her, I could understand why: both were still badly affected, more than a year after Collan Rex had been sent to prison.

So I wasn't expecting the message I got on 17 January from Angela. It was a forwarded message from Seth.

"I've decided I will talk to the author."

I asked Angela what had made him want to talk to me.

"I think it was the young boy who died."

And, of course, it was then that I realised that Enock had died two days previously. Another boy coming forward because of the death of a Grade 8, on camp with Parktown Boys'.

I met Seth a couple of days later at his home. His mom and sister were out. He was tall – I always marvel at how fast teenage boys grow. He was handsome, with a smile that split his face in two when he used it, and he had a lovely, personable manner. His mother was right. He was very upset about what had happened to Enock, and how the matrics on the camp were being spoken about. We were on the same page about that; I also thought the boys had been unjustly treated, expecially on social media, accused of initiations gone wrong (there were no initiations taking place, wrong or otherwise).

"Rex was the first person I met at Parktown Boys'," said Seth. "He was the first master I was ever introduced to because he was there on orientation day. He was a really nice guy; he shook my hand and shook my dad's hand and signed me in and right away he seemed to be a super chilled master. In school, there is always going to be that strict master who is all about the rules, and then there's a chilled master who lets you get away with stuff. He was more of a mate than a master to a lot of boys. I mean, even when it developed into where he would fight with us ... That's where that master/student barrier should be in place, but with Rex it wasn't there. So when all these things started happening, they weren't just happening to me, they were happening to others all around me and never once did I think, this shouldn't be happening, or that I was being molested. It never crossed my mind that it was wrong until he got arrested and even then I was like, 'No, I don't believe that that was his intent.' You could say Rex was my friend.

"I was supposed to go to another high school in Joburg. I had been at the junior school and I really wanted to go to the high school, pretty much 90 per cent of my grade was going and when I didn't get in, it was a massive shock. It felt like rejection. My mom even went to the GDE to get me a spot, because we were right there. Luckily, my dad was down – he works on a cruise ship so he's only here a few times a year, but when he is here, things get done. He said, 'Well, let's try a few schools,' and one of those was Parktown. I knew nothing about it, except that it was good at sport. So my dad said, 'Time's running out, let's send you to Parktown, into the hostel, because they always want boarders.' So he paid the deposit and I was, like, I'm a Parktown boy now. I wasn't that unhappy, because I did some research on Parktown, on the history and stuff, and when I got to Grade 8 I saw the workings of the school were fantastic. It sometimes sucked for Grade 8s, but what they were doing for Grade 8s was also good.

"First night the whole form had dinner and it was awkward because no one knew each other. And then all the matrics went into the hall and the Grade 8s were outside, and they'd call us to come in one at a time. Collan Rex was overseeing it. There was a chair on the stage and you'd come in and the matrics would shout 'Chair!' and you'd go up the stairs to the stage and they'd be like ... 'No, no, no, come down, come down, Chair!' and you'd have to climb on the stage without using the stairs. And they'd keep saying, 'Chair!' and you had to get up, get down, stand on the chair. Then you had to tell them your name and why you had come to Parktown. They asked us, 'What's the furthest you've been with a girl?', and you had to tell them and they'd say, 'Now demonstrate on the chair.' It's not nice obviously, but it's not bullying – it's not going to harm me. I understand how it could, but if you can't take that on the chin, you shouldn't be at a boys' school.

"Grade 8 was by far the best year I ever had at Parktown. Look, the camp was intense, I will say that. For example, the first night the matrics would call you to stand up in front of everyone and they'd say, 'Show us something you can do. Show us your talents,' and it was humiliating being up there because what talents do you really have at that stage? A lot of people were laughing at you, and people got upset when you laughed at them. But we were all going through it. I found it very bonding. The next morning the matrics came at 3 or 4 am and woke us up to go outside for push-ups and we had to hold push-up position for ages. And these are obviously not good things, but surviving them is good. I will never forget the words of the head of hostel at that camp. We were all doing push-ups and he said, 'You should love what you are doing right now. You are sweating and bleeding for your brothers and should be willing to do that.'

"Although Grade 8 camp was hard, we ended up so bonded and kids I was in school with then, I'd help them even now if I saw them on the street. I might not socialise with them after I finish school, but I will always be bonded to them.

"I was never afraid in Grade 8. Even my matric, he play-fought with me every day, but he wasn't trying to hurt me – he was trying to discipline me because I came into Grade 8 very cocky. I was slightly rebellious, but I was a good kid. My matric would say, 'Come now, let's fight,' and I'd say, 'No, I can't fight you,' and he'd say, 'If you don't fight me, it's going to be worse for you.' And I was like 50 kilograms and he was like 100 kilograms, but I loved him. As much as he beat me up and made me do things I didn't want to do, I still loved him.

"The worst thing I ever had to do was clean his fridge. It was horrible. I had been dreading it for weeks. It was so bad … There could have been a habitat in there and I had to ask Mrs Bossert for cleaning stuff to clean out my old pots' fridge, and she said, 'No, no let someone else do it.' So someone else cleaned it and he got super upset. And I said to him, 'Well, I wasn't trying to get out of it. I tried to clean it but ma'am said no.' But then ma'am bought them stuff for their fridge and everyone was okay. So I just had to do push-ups after that.

"But I never minded those things. Even when I got beat up, I genuinely believe that made me a better person. I think it's the problem with Parktown now; I can say to a Grade 8, please pick up that piece of paper, and if he says no, what must I do? I'm at that point in my school career where I still care and I would like to think I'm still a force in the hostel. I'll still say to kids if they're wrong, 'You're wrong – go do this,' and I'll be harsh.

"Like roll call; we stayed in Foundation in Grade 8 and that's quite a long way from Druce Hall where the matrics stayed. They gave us a 10 count and if one person in your form didn't make it then you all had to hold push-up position until roll call was over. Yes, it's bad and, yes, it's hard, but in those moments I've never felt closer to people, because all you have in common when you go back to your dorm is hating the matrics. So although it was a form of initiation, it didn't feel like initiation – it just felt like discipline.

"My whole point is that Grade 8 was good for me and it was good for our form, even when the matrics made you stand outside in your underwear at night in the cold. Obviously, it was kak. The matrics have got coffee and their robes on and they're chilling, watching us. Obviously, you don't want to be in that situation, but it's not the hardship that's important, but what the hardship does for you.

"One of my best memories in Grade 11 is a leadership camp; it's where they decide who is going to be a prefect. We did this race in teams, totally independent of teachers or guides, just you and a map and no instructors and you have challenges you have to overcome and you have to do all of them. So, like, we would build rafts and sail them into this freezing lake, then search around a mountain for an unmanned checkbox and then sign that we were there, and that alone took an hour to find. It was at the top of the mountain and it was difficult to get there. And this whole thing, the quickest team to finish was, like, 12, 13 hours. It was really intense while we were going through it; there were 12 in a group and four had dropped out by the time we got to the fourth activity. You were allowed to drop out, but the activities still had to be done, which meant those of us who were left, some of us had to do everything twice. I wanted to drop out, but I didn't; team morale was low, but we pushed ourselves and afterwards we felt so strong. I wanted to get through it and I did.

"I truly believe our form now, the matrics, is the only good form left in the school. And I'm going to try to change things with these Grade 8s for the better. It's the only thing I don't agree on with the Bosserts. I understand we have no right to make the Grade 8s do push-ups, but they should want to comply. Like, I took cadets last year; when I was in cadets, we had to do so many push-ups and run so many times even if one of us screwed up. It was blanket punishment. So if you turn wrong, everyone does push-ups or has to run. So then I told my Grade 8s to run 200 metres, because I thought I could. I mean, it's running, you know, and it's not even far; it's not like I was making them run to King Edward VII School. But Mr Bossert said, 'No, you can't do this.' So I said to the cadets, I said, 'Gents, if you guys screw up, I am going to make you run. Who doesn't want to run?' And everyone put their hand up. And then I said, 'Do you have a problem with me making you run?' And no one put their hand up. And I don't think it's because they feared me – I think it was because they respected me. I'm the kind of person who, if you respect me, I will treat you with respect. And I never hit people.

"With the Rex thing, I never thought it was wrong. I thought, to me, it was how it was and I had to accept it. Hardships fall under the same category for me. So with him, when it moved from choking and wrestling to groping, I didn't realise it; I was seeing it all as the same thing. If it was just happening to me, then maybe I would have noticed, but it was happening to all the boys. I never played waterpolo myself, but no one made a big deal about it in the water, and I think no one spoke out because [Rex] was seen as a friend at the end of the day. I didn't see him as molesting me; I saw it as just us playing around. I didn't like it – no one likes that sort of thing – but it becomes, like, part of the process. Like when Rex would come into our dorms and want to fight a bunch of us and we had to dive through beds and stuff – that was fun, it wasn't uncomfortable. So when everyone else is laughing, it seems like a game. As much as it's uncomfortable, it doesn't faze you.

"I only found out Rex was arrested the day afterwards because I wasn't at school at the time; I was home sick and a friend sent me a message saying, 'Dude Rex got arrested.' And then my mom came to me and said Rex had got arrested and asked me if he had done anything to me and I said no, because I was doing my best to defend him because at the time, in my eyes, he was being wrongly convicted. I liked him – he was my friend. I never saw Rex as an enemy, not that whole year. Until it got serious and people were going to court and then I started thinking about it and I thought, well, why would he do that?

"Jonah was my Grade 9 friend when I was in Grade 8. He would help me with my homework, and he would talk to me. He was my only friend in a higher grade and we were close. I didn't even know he had left the school until I saw him just after that, on holiday in Cape Town. I was there with my dad, and he asked me if Jonah was part of the case as well. I didn't know and my dad wasn't going to ask him what had happened or what his view was. At that time, I wasn't sure I was going to testify. So I talked to Jonah and it was very intense and I said, 'So, I'll see you at school,' and he said, 'No, I'm going to another school.' I realised he wasn't leaving because he wanted to go to another school – he was leaving because of Rex.

"I thought about it quite a lot. What bugged me most was, why didn't it seem like there was malicious intent? Why did it seem like it was just another day at the office? It didn't seem like he was trying to molest us – it was just him and his personality. It never seemed like he was groping you for his pleasure; I didn't think that was his intent. And I couldn't get that out of my head.

"I only once had a moment when Rex grabbed my genitals and lifted me up and then I was kind of, like, okay, this is not cool. But I never thought of telling anyone that this wasn't right; I never thought about reporting it, because it didn't seem like a reportable issue. When I heard about the video, then it became a different story, especially when I heard that it was Jonah. I was very heartsore and I thought, this is a lot more serious than I thought it was. And maybe Rex was a bad guy.

"When I heard he went to jail and my mom kept asking, 'Did anything happen to you?' I said no, because I knew if I said yes, I would have to testify and at that time I didn't want to because, yes, he was doing those things, but I don't think with malicious intent. It took me a couple of months to see it differently. One of the Grade 11s helped me to open up a lot, because he was so kind to me, which higher grades usually aren't. And because he was friendly to me he was easier to trust.

"I love the Bosserts. You can ask my mom – they're like my second family, and as much as I could go and speak to them, it was so much easier to speak to [my friend in Grade 11]. He would come and talk to a few of us, once or twice a week before bedtime, and say, 'Do you want to talk about it?' and I would say, 'These things did happen to me,' but I still didn't think Rex was in the wrong. Eventually, I told him everything that happened and I said I can understand why it's wrong, but I still don't want to testify, and he said, 'Just think about it.' And I thought about it and then went to speak to Mrs Bossert and I told her I would testify. And I did.

"I remember the thing I was most upset about was going to court. Testifying was one of the hardest days of my life because I had to tell a bunch of people, in detail, what happened to me. So it was really difficult and, like I said, I'd tried to forget as much as possible. Just before we went in, the prosecutor let me read my statement and that brought up a lot of emotions and then I had to go and say those things. In my statement, I said it happened 10 to 12 times and when I was in court I said 12 to 15 times, and they said, 'That's not the right number,' and then my court case was thrown out. I thought everything I'd been through was for nothing. I had had to remember everything for nothing. I thought that was unfair. By then my opinion of Rex had changed; I thought, I don't want what happened to me to happen to anyone else. So I thought, let me try put my nail in that coffin. I didn't want to testify for me and I wasn't trying to hurt Rex; I was just trying to protect other people from him and maybe my testimony would make a year or two years' difference.

"When I heard he was going to prison for 23 years, I thought he would commit suicide. If that was me, I would have committed suicide, because what life would you have to live in prison and when you got out, who would employ you? I thought he was going to get less, so when I heard he got more, I thought, okay, well, cool. But I do think it should have been a life sentence because I feel like those people don't change and he shouldn't be allowed out again.

"I don't know how I've dealt with it. I don't want to say it's affected me that much, because there was that period of time when it was nothing, when it didn't matter. But then it did matter and, as soon

119

as it did matter, I didn't want it to matter. I did my best to forget it and I think I've done a pretty good job of that. If you were to hand me my affidavit that the police first took down, there would probably be a lot of things I've forgotten because I've tried to force myself to remember. I don't want to remember. It doesn't have to be part of my future. So I try my best to forget it – and then I do. I mean, it's pretty intense, but I don't think it's something that's going to define my life at all, because I've pushed it down and even when Mrs Bossert took me to a therapist, I tried to avoid speaking about it. I'd rather talk about other problems in my life. Speaking about what happened made it worse because it made it seem much more real.

"I think I would try my best to avoid seeing Rex again. I don't think confronting him would do me any good. I don't hold any animosity against him; I don't hate him at all. I don't think of him as a molester, just a person I wouldn't want in my neighourhood. The school was put in a very bad light and it wasn't the school's fault at all. I would send my kids to Parktown. Parktown is a proud, character-building school and it's full of tradition and history."

Chapter 14
The Boy in the Video
*Jonah

I didn't expect to hear back from *Sharon when I messaged her. I had had her number since the end of 2019, but I couldn't call it. I didn't know how to ask her if I could talk to her or to her boy. At one point, I thought I would message her to explain why I wasn't going to message her, that I didn't want to be responsible for dredging up old pain and opening old wounds, especially as I didn't know whether they had gone any way towards healing. But, as more and more parents and boys came forward, I realised I owed it to her and to her son to at least ask.

She came back to me almost immediately. Yes, both her and Jonah would like to talk. And, yes, I could meet them at their home.

When I arrived, Jonah was warm and welcoming. Sharon was shaky. She started to cry before we sat down and I wondered again if I was asking too much.

"No," she said. "It's time," she reassured me.

"When Enock Mpianzi died in January, earlier this year, on a Grade 8 camp, my heart just broke. There was no supervision. Where were those teachers? There were no senior people looking after those boys. It was so unnecessary to lose a life.

"The death of this young boy and the whole Collan Rex tragedy just makes me want to force parents to wake up! Do not sit and condone this. Can this code of silence just come to an end now? Can the men, the fathers of these boys, stand up and have the courage to say, 'This is *not* okay'? When Enock drowned, I cannot tell you what it did to me, to my son Jonah and to his sister. It just churned up all the trauma of that very camp, that my boy, Jonah, attended as a little Grade 8, thinking he was starting a wonderful bright future at his new school. It churned up all that emotion, the memory of the pain and agony inflicted on all our boys."

In a previous interview, one of the mothers had asked, "Does someone have to die before our boys are taken seriously?" And, listening to Sharon, this came flooding back to me. Because somebody had died.

Sharon continued.

"I've always said to Jonah, 'You have to speak the truth.' Those boys whose fathers were Old Boys, those boys will not tell you the truth. Those men condone the culture of violence; it's shut them up and kept them quiet. That code of silence at Parktown Boys' runs very deep. There were masters who were part of it. They created the illusion that the school was a safe place; we were led to believe that it was a wonderful establishment with healthy traditions. There was a time that those traditions worked and I miss those traditions terribly and Jonah misses them too. But why would certain people believe that they needed to break these boys to such a state, mentally and physically? Shouldn't school be an environment where we build these boys up?

"I was put into such awkward situations at the headmaster's office many a time. I probably went in there at least five times a year, and I was shut down every time. It was as if the whole culture was saying, 'What woman comes here and challenges the school?' I would complain about a number of things. I'd say, 'You have one master in prep caretaking 13 boys, while my son stands guard at the door. Watching a door. What is the purpose of that, what's the reason behind that? What kind of culture are we breeding?' There were so many times I raised these issues at the school. I challenged them, but they shut me down. I said, 'My son's marks are pathetic, something is wrong here. What is happening while these boys are in prep?' In my opinion, this culture was condoned by all those housemasters – they were smooth operators, smooth and charming. Every Sunday night, a housemaster would be there, waiting for the parents so that he could schmooze them. 'Look at your son, he's becoming a man, he's become so confident.' Many a Sunday night I heard those same lies. And I will never forget them. Never. Never.

"On Fridays, I would go to Parktown Boys' and load these boys up to take them home for the weekend. Rob and Jonah, they would all pass out in the car. It would take hours to drive home down Jan Smuts, and they would sleep all the way. I raised this with their parents and said, 'Something's wrong.' But I couldn't talk to some of those parents; their ears were closed, hoping it would go away. But Rob's mom, such a lovely woman, she listened. She was also always at the school, fighting for those boys."

"How did you feel when Jonah told you he wanted to go to boarding school?" I asked. I could see how tight-knit this family was. It seemed incomprehensible that she would have been okay with it. And she hadn't been.

"My heart broke the day my 13-year-old son went to boarding school. I've questioned myself so many times. Why was I so gullible to let him go to a boarding house? As a single mother, raising a son, with no father figure in his life, I thought this would be a positive and uplifting environment for him to learn how to be a man, a good man in society, with good manners and integrity.

"I constantly asked about initiation practices. I questioned them. I was the big mouth. I made sure I was on the committee because I wanted to help improve the boarding house, because that place was a dump when we got there. Myself and other parents were committed to do as much fundraising as possible to uplift the environment. I stood at the entrance to the corporate offices' car parks and raised funds for that school. I wanted to see the good in it, and contribute because I believed that the school was good. It had a good name in the past.

"There were certain Old Boys and masters who were very opposed to any new ideas; they were intent on protecting 'the Parktown way'. At meetings and AGMs, they would always try to buck any new ideas – new was not going to fly there.

"It felt like the principal had lost control of his staff and the school. The same old excuse was given over and over again: 'Old school traditions, we have to uphold these traditions.' But they had lost the plot. Their traditions weren't about building up these boys – they were all about breaking them down.

"In Grade 8, I attended a parents' evening because I was worried about Jonah. For the first few months, he was wobbling, but he wouldn't say why. I kept reaching out to him to say, 'Look, you've been put in this school. Let's give it a year, because to just take you out midway isn't a solution.' I asked him if we could just try to get through the first year.

"That night I tried to find him at the boarding house, but I couldn't. When I was leaving the school, I saw he had left a note on my car. It was something to the effect of 'Get me out of here', or 'Can I come home?' I got a terrible feeling. I wish I had listened to my boy back then and taken him out that night. When I picked him up that Friday, I tried to reassure him. I said, 'Yes, this would be the easy way to opt out, but tell me what's going on.' ‹Nothing, Mom.' That's all he said. So I said, 'Well, let's get through the year.' And then it became silence. At the end of the year, I asked him, 'Are you fine? Are you staying, or do you want to come home?' And he just said, 'No, Mom, it's going to be okay.' But it never was okay.

"If only I had trusted my instincts. If only the boys had felt able to tell their parents what was going on. But how could they? How do you report as abnormal something that seems normal to every other grade in the school? And especially at 13, no one is confident that they are going to know better. Especially when the masters seem so on board with it.

"But then Mariolette and Chris Bossert arrived at the school. It was such a relief. I knew then that it was going to turn around for the good. They had come from reputable schools with solid track records of what they had instilled in boarding-house establishments. They immediately went about drastically improving things. The amount they did for that school, we're all so indebted to them. They did so much for our boys. They turned the boarding house into a state-of-the-art establishment. And Jonah was much happier once the Bosserts arrived, and also when Grade 8 was over."

"When did you first suspect something wasn't right with Collan Rex?" I asked. "Or didn't you?"

Sharon's eyes filled with tears again.

"I knew there was something wrong, Sam," she said. "I just didn't know what. Until that waterpolo trip when Jonah was in Grade 9.

"I had a bad feeling from the start. I really didn't want Jonah to go. I don't know what got over me. I just had this feeling because I'd watched Rex interact with him at a waterpolo match, pushing him and hugging him. These hugs kept playing over and over in my mind. They just didn't feel okay. They felt too tight, too familiar. So I said, 'No, you are not going on that trip, end of story.' But Rex called me, and messaged me repeatedly. 'Oh, ma'am,' he said, 'it will be so good for Jonah. It will help him to get into the first team. He's showing such potential.' He told me it would build my son's progress and all that BS. It almost felt like, if I didn't send him, he wouldn't get into the first team, and I'm sure that, as a young boy, well, everyone aspires to get onto the top team. So after all these messages I was left thinking that if I didn't give him the opportunity, I would be depriving my boy, that he had all this potential and he really wanted to go. But I continued to say no to Rex. Every time I saw him at the waterpolo, he would ask me if I'd changed my mind. He literally wore me down. Eventually, I thought, dammit, let him just go! I just can't take any more of this Rex – the messages were intense.

"But deep down I knew.

"Jonah left for Durban. I never heard from him that entire weekend. I assumed it was because he was so busy. But when he came home, no underpants came home. To be honest, most weekends there were no undies in his washing. I thought, what the hell! Why aren't they coming home? Where are the underpants? It really felt like something was not okay. I'd often ask him about this, and he'd simply say he'd washed his undies in the shower. But I knew. Something wasn't right."

Something wasn't right, but Sharon didn't know exactly what, and Jonah certainly wasn't talking. He might never have said anything if Ben hadn't gone to the Bosserts. It might still have been going on even now. I asked her about the phone call she got from Mariolette on 3 November 2016.

"The night the school called me to tell me about what had happened with Collan Rex it was raining very hard. Initially, they wouldn't tell me the reason for the call; they just told me that I had to come to the school immediately. Imagine the trauma? A mother gets called to the school and she is given no reason why! I had no idea what was wrong, whether he was hurt or if he had done something wrong, if he had got into drugs. I raced there. I managed to make it there in 20 minutes in the rain, not knowing what was going on. When I finally heard what had happened, all I could think about was my traumatised child and why I hadn't listened to my instincts and taken him out of this school. It was devastating. The SGB head left me to go to Hillbrow police station all on my own. He insisted I went alone. I was so distraught. I asked Chris Bossert to accompany me and thankfully he did.

"When we got to the police station, Rex was there too. He literally sat there on the floor with his phone in his hand. As soon as I saw him, I said to the charge officer, 'Take that phone out of his hands!' I was so angry ... I could have ... You don't want to know. It was *this* close. My daughter was also there, telling me to calm down. I often think what I would do if I was on the road and he was coming towards me ... The last image I have of him is him sitting there on the floor of the police station, reading messages from my son, sending messages to my son. The worst thing was when he said to me, 'Can I

125

please explain to you?' I said through clenched teeth, 'There's nothing to explain.' I just wanted to attack him but something in me said, just calm down and write your statement.

"Then, as I was writing the statement, this charge officer started saying to me, 'Stop writing like that – you're doing it wrong!' He said I needed to write to the end of the page and I thought, wow, I could hit you right now. My daughter came and stood behind me and said, 'Calm down, Mom.'"

"In the moment, that was good advice," I said to Sharon. "But how do you ever calm down from something like this? What do you do when you get home from the police station? What happens then?"

Sharon nodded.

"After something like this happens, I don't think you are ever okay, even when you go for counselling. Jonah went to a forensic psychologist, who had seen him before the court case, on 13 June 2017. I think it was worth every minute of those three hours because it really helped him. I never knew what happened in their session, but when I came to pick him up, she asked to speak to me alone. All she said was, 'Please give Jonah space. Please. Back the fuck off.' But, I thought, I can't! I have to protect him now because I have failed him as a mother. But then I tried to listen to her. This woman was an expert – she knew what she was doing. And I managed to convince myself to step back.

"When I was looking for a new school for Jonah, I was open with all the principals I saw. I told them what had happened. I said to them, 'I'm not going to sugarcoat this. I have a son who is broken, in pieces. Please be honest with me, will you consider looking at his situation? Here's his report. You can't judge him on this, you can't even look at these marks – 20 per cent, 30 per cent … You can't base his performance on your academic ethos. And if you say no to me, well …'

"My heart was broken. I felt so alone in the world. Everyone was turning us away and closing doors.

"I said to my son, 'Jonah, you are broken, broken, you are shattered in pieces.'

"A few months ago I spoke to a colleague who had just placed her son in Parktown boarding. I said, 'I had a bad experience with Parktown, but that doesn't mean you will have one too. But I would like to tell you my story and I would like to give you two or three triggers to look for. If your son is sleeping in the car on a Friday afternoon, shutting down on the Sunday when you take him back to boarding school, if there's a disconnect, then you have to be worried.'

"When I look back, my son was so disconnected. I used to say to him, 'You're here, but you're not here.' He was in a black hole so deep. So deep.

"Talking out about this has been very healing. When the charges were read, it was the first time I knew the extent of that child's abuse. We got to a stage when Jonah said no more psychologists. He said, 'Mom, I've got my aunts, and I've got my sister.' He confides in his sister more now than ever before. He did, however, agree to go for further counselling, which has been of tremendous value and helped with his healing.

"When Enock died, Jonah fell apart. I sat him down and said, 'Okay, this has now happened. We can't deny it's affected us. It's affected all of us, but we have to stand up and speak. You've been in court; you spoke your truth. It was an ordeal you wish on no one, but your voice was heard. Your charges were read.'

"And, talking about it now, I feel empowered. I feel a calm. I told Jonah that this is a chapter we need to close before we can move forward. So we both decided to speak out. These days we have such a close bond and that's all that's kept us moving forward. It's never going to be okay and there's scarring for life, but through all of this, we've tried to see the debris and walk through it. It's brought us even closer together."

Jonah has his own thoughts about what happened, how it happened, and the mark it has left – on him, and his mother Sharon.

"I remember the day I found out I was the one in the video. The thing about that video is that I don't think I was the worst affected; I was just the one who was the main focus of it. I know one of the other boys got dragged into the next room, but I can't share what happened there – that's his story. I'm fine to speak about what happened to me. That video, though, it showed what actually was going on.

"We had a waterpolo match that day at Affies, and we came back to school, but Rex then asked us if we could play club waterpolo at Zoo Lake. While we were waiting to go, we were chilling in the common area, and that's where all of that stuff happened. In a way, I am grateful it was seen. Very grateful. Otherwise, none of this would have come out.

"That evening, before I found out someone had reported it, I was worried because the whole time I could see my mom's car in the parking area. I asked Collan, 'Do you know why my mother's here?' He didn't and started asking around. Then he told me that it was just a meeting. But much later, I walked down onto the field and my mom was there with my sister and they were both crying and saying, 'We are here for you.'

"Then later on we were lying in bed and the one boy sent us a message to say the police had arrived and we were all, like, 'What's going on? Someone's getting into trouble ...' And then they saw Collan being taken away in handcuffs. Then we heard the knock on the door and we thought we were all going to be arrested. The matron Mariolette came in and said to me, 'Pack your bags, let's go.' I was very confused and worried.

"I messaged Rex. I even remember when I messaged him – I was sitting in the Bosserts' house after Mariolette had called me and I sent Rex a message asking what was happening, because he was the only one who would know. When it came to court, thinking about that was the most stressful thing, because I thought, oh no, they're going to question me about messaging him. The court was definitely the most traumatising thing about all of it.

"I had convinced my mom to let me go to boarding school. I had a friend down the road who went to Parktown Boys' and he told me all the stories about it and it sounded amazing. I wanted to go because I haven't had my dad in my life to raise me. I've only had my mom and my sister, and I've never seen how males interacted with each other I thought it would be cool.

"We got there in January 2015, a day before school started, and went on camp the following day. I was very excited, because it was, like, you don't even go to school, you just go on camp! I'd been on camp at a different school in Grade 7 and it was so cool, so I was really looking forward to it. I had great expectations.

"But it was very different to what I expected. We got to this camp and the matrics called us and made us get into a huge circle and said, 'Push-up position!' We had to do that for about two hours. They also made us do other exercises like squats and stuff, but push-ups are the ones I remember. After lunch there were more push-ups, which by then felt like torture. I remember dinner was at about 6 or 7pm and after that we did more push-ups until midnight. And then the matrics woke us up at 3am for war cries and more push-ups. We also had to sleep outside; we just had our sleeping bags and our arm as a pillow.

"I remember my back hurt so much. You would sit down, but you couldn't hold yourself up so you would just fall backwards. I wasn't the fittest back then; I was quite chubby.

"None of that made me form bonds with anyone from my group in camp – that only happened when we got back to hostel. I was stressed about going back to hostel. While we were on camp, they were telling us that we were the worst people and back at school we would be made to do even more push-ups, so I was very scared. They built up their reputations with threats and all that. The matrics were very scary. Once back at boarding, after roll call and before lights out, they would make us wait and hit us, once each, with a stick as we went to bed. My old pot punched me and degraded me in the first half of the year, but he became a good guy about halfway through the year and then he protected me and didn't hit me any more.

"When the Bosserts arrived to run boarding, it made everything a thousand times better. All the way through Grade 8 I kept telling my mom I wanted to leave. When they arrived, everything improved – just little things, like getting a cake on your birthday; it was the happiest thing ever. You could share it with your dorm and that made it better. Also, the following year, in Grade 9, you got more privileges and you never had to worry about your matrics any more.

"When I first met Collan I saw him as a friend, as one of the hostel boys. He was young, like one of us. He used to go buy us cigarettes. I think only when I got to leave Parktown and everything came out in court, did I properly acknowledge the whole situation: that he actually wasn't one of our friends, that these weren't just harmless games.

"The Durban waterpolo trip was when everything escalated. We were on tour to Durban High School. It was only the under-16s who were supposed to go, but some of them got pulled up to first team, so some of us under-15s got called to go with. Durban is where it got really bad. I know for one of my school friends, Ben, it was pretty rough because of the stuff Rex did to him. And it was after that that Ben made sure the Bosserts saw the video that got Rex arrested.

"I can't tell you exactly how many times it happened to me. I remember, at night he would come into the dorm room and we would lock our door because we were scared he would come in, but he would unlock our doors with his key. Then he would come in while we were trying to sleep and start wrestling with us and stuff. He would grab our penises when we were playing waterpolo – he said it was to toughen us up. It happened whenever he jumped into the pool with us.

"It's tough now because I've tried to shove everything down, so I don't remember everything, but I do remember it happened quite a few times. Then it got more violent. There's this little room called the ball cage, where all the waterpolo balls were kept, and you had to put them back after practice. One day I was in there, packing stuff away, the other boys were still around, and then Rex came in behind me and started fondling me and cupping my genitals and dry humping me. He also hit me and then he went out, got the keys and slammed the door, and put the keys just out of my reach and said, 'Get the keys.' That was quite traumatising for me. It was really hard because all the boys were laughing and you had to stay strong. Rex did pick on some of us more than others. Rob and I were good friends, so we told each other stuff. We spoke about how some of us boys were getting picked out at school. I tried to reassure him because he was very vulnerable. We used to be close.

"Rex never seemed to mind about the cameras. We all knew they were there. I remember, when we were all lying there and we would say to him, 'Rex, the camera is pointing at you,' and he would move the boy he was hurting away and then just continue.

"I think a lot of us went into a deep depression during this time. My mom took me to the doctor and I went on to antidepressants. I took them while I was there, but as soon as I left the school I stopped taking them. I remember being constantly tired. I disconnected from everyone, but not intentionally. My mom would say, even my aunt could tell you, that I was always smiling when I was young, but when I went to Parktown I slowly started pulling away, withdrawing.

"I've had bad dreams at night. I remember once I heard screaming and I thought Rex had broken into our house and was harming my mom and sister and I ran into their room screaming. It happened a few times.

"If I had to see Rex again? I'm past that now ... I've accepted it. In my mind, it's over. The court case took such a long time, and was such a burden. Every time I thought, okay, it's over now and I'm out of Parktown – I had begun growing and doing well at my new school – then they would come to the house and say, 'This is when you have to go to court,' and it would be like starting all over again.

"During this time my mom asked me if I wanted to leave and I said yes. The new school was my turning point. It took some getting used to. It's weird [because] you get different types – in Parktown, you get the richest of the rich and the poorest of the poor, but we were all friends. In my new school, it was harder. I didn't have fancy shoes or an iPhone but my friends really took me under their wings and I'm grateful for that. If I didn't go there... I don't know where I would be now.

"It also helped that I've somehow managed to accept that all of this was my story and that if I wanted to share it then it must be shared. So rather than people finding out, I decided I would share it with the people I felt comfortable with. So all my closest friends, I've told them my story and, if they don't like it, well they must get out. But they've stayed. I'm in a good place. It's a good place. I feel like this whole thing with Collan has really moulded me into how I show myself in the world today. Am I proud of myself? I am proud of myself."

Chapter 15
Reflections

In all of this, I kept coming back to two things I found incomprehensible. The first was that the boys had seen being molested as part of life at school, just another hardship to be endured alongside knuckle push-ups and standing outside in the cold. None of them had recognised it as a deviance, something to be reported. And why would they, when they weren't encouraged to report beatings, or lack of food or long-term physical damage? When people asked later why, if it was so bad, they hadn't come forward, it blew my mind that they couldn't see that the boys hadn't come forward for precisely that reason. Anyone who has seen a movie about a bank robbery knows that even if there are 20 hostages on the ground, they all bow to the one person carrying a gun.

"They were boys, they were strong, they could have fought him off," was an oft-heard opinion. They were children, he was an adult and already they had learned that right or wrong at school depended on who was giving the instruction. And being silent secured survival of sorts.

The second element that struck me was the divide between what the boys told their parents and what actually happened. While the likes of Ben told his father almost every detail, there were still things his father only discovered during our interview. Others couldn't face seeing the reaction on the faces of their fathers in particular. So many mothers and fathers had to leave it up to their own imagination as to what had happened under the covers, in the locker room, in the prep hall and in the pool. And, for some, the reality might have been easier to deal with than the nightmare.

I remember when I was little, my father going away and turning to my brothers, both of whom were younger than me, and telling them they needed to "look after Mummy and Sam," because they were now "the men of the house".

From an early age, we teach our boys that they have a duty as a protector. But what's left of them if they cannot even protect them-selves?

Chapter 16
The Woman in Black
Jolene

By now, I had heard a lot about Collan Rex. I had heard how nice he was and how disgusting he had been and how kind he could be and how conflicted the boys – and, in some cases, even their parents – were about the sentence.

I really needed to speak to Collan. And so I called Jolene. She is his girlfriend and has been with him since halfway through the trial, since August 2018. I had seen photographs of her outside court, a young woman with dark hair and eyes and a jaw that was permanently set. Walking into court with her head held high, always in black, she seemed bulletproof. She didn't smile much, and if she did, the cameras never caught it. She testified on Collan's behalf during the sentencing.

When I checked her Facebook page, I saw a lot of photos of the two of them together. She looked like an entirely different person on social media, and for that matter, so did he. Collan had gone from what appeared to be a fairly jovial person in school photographs, to quite thug-like in appearance. He had put on weight. Many pictures were taken of him outside the courthouse wearing a suit that I didn't think was his usual wardrobe. He looked ill at ease in it, a far cry from the tracksuited waterpolo coach beaming in team pictures.

Jolene was at court a lot, more so than Collan's family. His grandfather stayed in the carpark during the trial, and his mom was absent a great deal of the time, including for the actual sentencing. Jolene, however, was there.

In Facebook photographs, the two of them look years younger, like teenagers. They are smiling and joyous; there is a real sense of happiness and contentment about them, as though neither have a care in the world. You would never guess that they met after he went on trial, and that much of their relationship would be played out on the steps of the Palm Ridge courthouse.

I was very curious about Jolene. Talking about her provoked pretty extreme reactions from the people to whom I had spoken: Mariolette Bossert, the Archivist and a few from Bikers Without Bullies.

"She's got a child herself!" Mariolette said, angry and bewildered. "Doesn't she understand what he did? Doesn't she see he could hurt her child?"

The Archivist had spoken to Jolene directly after the sentencing.

"I saw her standing there and I went up to her and said something like, 'At least now you know your child will be safe,'" he said.

The prosecutor, Arveena Persad, had hammered that point home when cross-examining Jolene during the sentencing. Persad asked Jolene whether Collan had told her about his convictions. Jolene replied that he had said he had been accused of sexual assault and she could look it up if she wanted to but, she said, she had had nothing to do with it. And when Persad pressed the point that she had a five-year-old child, she stuck to her guns and said again that it was nothing to do with her.

The general opinion was that either Jolene was very stupid or an uncaring mother. I didn't consider either of those to be true. No one is that cold. I saw a young woman in an impossible situation. I wondered what she had seen in Collan that no one else had. So I reached out to her and called her at work.

"Hello?" she said cautiously.

"Hello, do you have a moment to chat?"

"About what?"

I tried to lighten the mood.

"Don't worry, I'm not trying to sell you a cell phone contract."

Silence.

"I'm writing a book about ..."

"I knew it!" She was angry.

"No, you don't know it," I said. "It's not what you think and I've been working on this long enough now to know what you probably think."

"Okay, so if it's not what I think, then what is it?"

"I'm writing a book about what happened at Parktown in 2016 from the perspective of the people who were there at the time. All of the people. Including Collan. Including you."

"Why me?" She sounded very suspicious.

"Because I think you've been victimised as much as anyone else here," I said. "And I don't think that's right."

She was quiet for a minute.

"I was. Do you know what people said to me? They said I should have my child taken away from me. They told me I should die."

"I know. And that's wrong."

"I love my child more than anything. *Anything*," she said fiercely.

"I believe you. I feel the same way."

Pause.

"Look, have coffee with me," I said. "I'll bring my recorder and if, afterwards, you change your mind, I'll erase the interview."

"I'm not ashamed or embarrassed about anything." I detected a slight sharpness in her voice. "You can bring your recorder and ask your questions."

We met at a quiet restaurant near to where Jolene lived in Krugersdorp. She was on a church fast, so she had water with lemon and I had coffee. She was prettier in life than in pictures, her face softer, and she looked much younger. But all the electricity was there under the surface.

"I am not going to bad-mouth Collan. I love him," she announced. "Collan is a good person who did wrong things."

"I didn't think you would."

"So I suppose you want to organise to see him."

"Yes, I would like to very much," I said. "But it's you I'm here to see now."

She wasn't sure she believed me.

"People always say that, but they just want to get to Collan."

"Well, I want to talk to you," I said firmly. "And then I will ask you at the end if you trust me and, if you do, I'll ask you to ask Collan to trust me too."

It was a gamble and I knew it. She might not have trusted me at all. But with her, as with everyone, I was as upfront as possible.

"Okay, well, we'll see," she said.

"Does Collan know about the drowning on the camp?" I asked.

"The Grade 8 camp?"

She nodded.

"Yes, we talked about it. It was actually a surprise when I saw it on the news about that kid who drowned ... The first thing Collan said to me was that's the same place they sent him; it's the same thing they did to him – the same thing ... It's like it's carrying on, it's not stopping. It's going to carry on and it's going to get worse."

She was upset. I changed the subject.

"Tell me about yourself," I said. "Tell me where you came from."

She nodded.

"Okay, let me tell you more about myself, then I can deal with the rest, okay. When I was eight years old, I was molested by a family friend. He was a friend of my grandmother, who I was staying with at the time. My mom had just dropped me off there – she did that a lot. It went on for quite a long time, and nobody noticed anything because every time I said I don't want this happening, and told him I wanted him to stop, he threatened me with a gun, or used to threaten me by saying my parents weren't going to believe me … you know, the normal thing that molesters do. So because I was a victim as a child I know exactly how victims react, and I know how people that do harm react."

"Did you ever tell anyone?" I asked.

"No. My grandmother found out though … And then he got, like, 10 years' house arrest or something. He never went to actual prison – not until much later."

"Later?"

She nodded.

"When I was 19 I met this guy again. I went back to Chrissiesmeer, where my grandmother lived; it was a short while, just before she was murdered. I went back to my grandmother's house."

"Your grandmother was murdered?" I was stunned and incredulous. "What happened?"

"I'll tell you just now. After I finish telling you about this guy. He was still there. I made friends with his wife. She knew about the story, but she didn't know I was the girl. So she knew about everything. He had told her, and obviously he knew it was me, but she never knew I was the girl. I didn't want to tell her that, because I was saving her from pain. It hurts, okay … So I never told her. And then one day we were at a braai and this girl, the daughter of her sister who had passed away, who was 13, she came to me after the braai and told me she wants to go home with me. She doesn't want to go home with them. I said, 'No, go home with them,' because it had been a long time ago and I thought maybe he was different. The next morning she phoned me. It was, like, very early, and she said to me, 'Jolene, I need to speak to you.' So I knew it. I knew he'd done it again. When I got to her, she told me he'd touched her and done this and that. I knew it, the way she was explaining it to me, it was exactly what he'd done to me. So I was 19 and I had to face this man in court again. It turned out he was doing it to other girls as well – I thought I was the only one. But this time I had to go to court."

She sipped her water.

"So I know what that's all about. I know these kinds of things ... I've been through it. I've been through court cases, more than enough."

"Like your grandmother's murder?" I asked.

"Exactly. I used to be there at the court every single time; the man who killed her, I knew him. He stayed by my grandmother. And he got 15 years. They found him sitting next to her body – he didn't even run away; he bathed her and put her back in bed, after killing her. We still don't know why. I would like to go to him and speak to him about it, but it's taken me quite a while to get to that point, because I've been through a lot after that."

It sounded to me as though Jolene had been through a lot already. I said so. She agreed.

"I went haywire after my grandmother's murder. I lived for my grandmother – she was my everything. And then after she died I started taking drugs, drinking, fighting a lot, going out. But I didn't mix with a lot of people. I knew everybody, and everyone knew me, because I'm very open and friendly and I'm a very, like, talkative person, so everyone knew me. Like, I went out ... I used to go from table to table in the clubs and greet everyone and speak to everyone. Then I came this side, back to Krugersdorp, about four or five years ago. I started working as a manager at the Dros."

The Dros.

In 2018, a man by the name of Nicholas Ninow raped a seven-year-old girl in the bathroom of a Dros restaurant in Silverton in Pretoria. He was jailed for life. Jolene saw my reaction. She laughed bitterly.

"Ja, that's exactly what the Parktown people also held against me. Someone said to me, ja, I've obviously just got a thing for rapists. I wasn't even at the Pretoria one – I was here by Krugersdorp. But it didn't matter. They made their own minds up."

"Tell me how you met Collan," I said gently.

She smiled widely.

"You know, for about two years we had the same friend group but we never met. So I went with this one friend to Sunset Rock [a club in Roodepoort] when it was still open ... This was now on 11 August 2018. I went with one of my friends, who it turned out was his friend as well, and I saw this guy. It was like he had this light around him, and I was, like, 'Wow!'"

She giggled.

"I nearly got over the table, who's this?! So I got this extreme exciting feeling, like, when I saw him. I was like, 'Wow! This ... wow! This guy, wow!'"

"It sounds like you were very excited," I said.

She nodded.

"And everyone says it's about his looks, and yes, he is a good-looking guy, but that wasn't it; there was something, there was potential. I saw something deeper. And then I walked past him in the club and he said, 'Jolene,' and I was like, 'Aagh! Oh my word, there goes my heart.' I definitely believe in love at first sight. Definitely. Most definitely, I do. So then I met him that night and the next day he wanted to come see me, and I said to him, 'No, it's church. No visitors on a Sunday.' So even though I used to still go clubbing and everything, church was a priority, I never used to skip church. I never used to miss it. So he came to see me on the Monday. He was all dressed nice and everything. When he visited, my heart broke for this man. I saw so much hurt in his eyes. I saw his heart – I didn't see Collan, I saw Collan's heart."

She laughed.

"When he first visited we stayed outside. I would rather visit with you outside on the stairs than let anyone come into my house and meet my child. I keep people away from my daughter. So when those Parktown people said I just let this person into my house, that upset me, because it was not true. Okay, me and him, we used to visit at my friend's house, but he never used to be in contact with my daughter at first. Not until I got to know him."

"Did you know at that time that he was on trial for molesting the boys?"

She shook her head.

"No, I didn't know anything. All I knew was how much I liked him and he liked me. We had been seeing each other for about two weeks when I went to Tzaneen with a friend who was staying with me. I was there for a week, but he was calling the whole time, saying to me that I needed to come home, that he needed to speak to me. His trial had started, but I never knew about it at that time."

"When was this?" I asked.

"This was 2018. He was sentenced in 2018. I met him just before he was sentenced, a few months before ... I met him in August. Then when I came and we went out, we sat in his car and then he told me."

"What did he tell you?" I really wanted to know.

"He said to me that he's busy with a court case, he's got ... then it was still 328 charges against him, this and this and this and this one.

He told me exactly what it was; he said to me, the accusations are sexual assault, rape – you know, the things like the bullying, the attempted murder, and all those kind of things. So I sat next to him in the car, and I smiled at him. I was like, 'This will blow over, don't worry.' He was petrified, you could say that. He got out of the car, and he said to me, 'If you want me to go, I will go. I won't be upset with you.' I got out and I walked up to him and looked at him, and those tears were running down his face, and I just kept looking at him and I was like, 'I'm not going anywhere.' I hugged him, and I said to him, 'Let's go make coffee.' And we went back into the house."

"And you never thought about leaving him?" I couldn't get my head around that. With that many charges of molestation and assault and rape? And attempted murder? She wasn't right on the number either – it was 387, not 327. But what's another 60-odd charges on 328?

She shook her head.

"Never."

She continued telling her story.

"Then I started going with him to court, and as soon as they knew I was the girlfriend, Parktown started attacking me, from all sides. They got my ex involved; they threatened me so many times. Once, it was on a Wednesday evening, and it was ten to seven, which I remember because I was at my church group, and I got a phone call from this lady, and this woman said to me she's a social worker. So I said to her that government closes at 4 pm, not at 7 pm, so why are you phoning? She said she wanted my address; she wanted to come meet me. She wanted to come evaluate my daughter because of this and this and this and this. I went to my pastor. I told him this, and they started praying. That woman never phoned me again. So ... then the next day I just sat and worried because these people were threatening me, who wanted my child taken away from me. One woman from the school started messaging me, and she also started messaging my mom. I've still got her messages. This woman opened up a page on Instagram and she started posting photos of me and Collan, saying, 'This is what a rapist does in his free time' and things like that."

"How did you stay sane?" I asked. "I don't think I would have. Do you have a lot of family support?"

She shook her head.

"I haven't, but that's okay. I'm very strong. Because I have God. When I first met Collan in the club I explained to him one thing. I'm a child of God, okay ... Because just after I met him, I stopped going out, I stopped drinking, I stopped doing everything that I was doing.

I said to him, 'Listen, I'm a mom, I go to church, I'm a huge Christian. This is what I'm busy with and I need to sort my life out, this is what is important to me, so you need to make a choice. If you carry on with your friends, your drinking, I'm out.'

"So, it stopped just there. He didn't even hesitate. Friday night, people used to phone us to come out. We were like, 'No, we're not interested, we're watching movies, leave us alone.' So we used to, like, me and him and my daughter, do pizzas, movies … We used to have fun. My child loves him – we all love him.

"I could tell Collan anything. So I spoke to him about my grandmother and I said to him, this is why I was so angry with God, because why did he allow this man to do this, and he didn't just kill her, he tortured her. It wasn't just a murder, it was like a brutal murder. Then he told me about his grandmother. When he was in matric, she died of cancer, on 11 August of his matric year. And his grandmother was as important to him as mine was to me. I have a tattoo with my grandmother's name, and the date that it happened, 13/11/13. And 11 is mine and Collan's number as well. The year 2013 my grandmother died, his grandmother died too. So there's a lot of things that connect me with Collan. It's not just about, oh, you fell in love, or whatever – there's a lot of things that connect us, a lot.

"So I can understand from his side that a person rebels when you get that hurt. People that get hurt hurt others. So if it's not dealt with in the right way, you go out and hurt … because you're hurt. You can't show love to people. That is a fact of life – you can't change that. When I spoke to Collan about my grandmother, he came out about his grandmother and then I related to that and that rebel stage. Then I said to him, 'Just come with me to church.' But he never wanted to. So the one day I was sitting on my bed, he was outside smoking, and I got this message from God, saying I must go and tell him that he remains a son of God, and God loves him. I went outside and I said to him, 'You know what, you remain God's son. He loves you and misses you, He wants you to come back home.' And that man broke. He cried and cried and cried and cried and he didn't stop. Then he said to me, 'Take me to church.' And so I did. That night at church he was so open for God to change his life. He was so, so, so open. You take people to church for the first time and they're usually very like closed, but he was open. His hands were up and he was praising and he was worshipping. It was something amazing. I didn't even worship … I was just looking at this man, like, wow! God's going to do great things with you. And Prophet Leon du Preez prayed for him and that man changed his life, like you cannot believe. I mean, Collan may be in prison, but he's serving in the church, he's preaching in the church. I promise you."

"I believe he was very close to his oupa as well," I said.

"He was. His poor oupa. I stayed by him for a while. He fell and I helped him up; I was there to assist him and everything. And he helped me a lot as well. He used to take Collan to court and everything. He loves Collan very much. He took me in when I didn't have a place to stay, just before Collan was sentenced. So in November 2018, I lost my job, I lost my place. My best friend shot himself on 22 November. And then on 29 November Collan was sentenced. So my November was hectic. It was hectic. In June last year I was still stuck in November. I was so traumatised with November. Even afterwards, even into this year, when I used to write a date, I'd end up writing November 2018, because I was still stuck there."

"Were you ever scared about what people would say to you at court? For a lot of people Collan was a pariah, a paedophile."

She gave me a look.

"That is unfair, it's very unfair. Collan is not the monster everyone's making him out to be. They made him out to be something that he's not. One of the bikers used to say nasty stuff to me. He's a 'biker against bullies', but he's the biggest bully of them all. The things they said about me, they hurt so much. They told me they were going to beat him up and stop him having children; they said I was a bad mother and they would have my daughter taken away. You know what, I understand these people are going through hurt, I understand these kids are going through hurt, but there's a way of dealing with things. You can't get a whole biker gang to a court case. I mean, I could have destroyed the man that killed my gran, I could have destroyed him. I've got the people to do it, I've got the connections to do it. I can destroy someone ... there's no problem in it. But that's not what a person does. When I walked into that court, those bikers were planning on hitting him, they were planning on kicking him between his legs so he could never have kids. I was just praying and praying ... I was like, God, no one will touch this man. But while I was praying I was thanking God already for his protection, knowing that no one would touch him. And, you know, till this day, everybody's hoping for it, but no one has touched Collan in jail. No one has touched him."

Jolene really did take the brunt of the anger from parents and supporters alike. Collan was in the court, but his girlfriend was outside and she was a soft target.

"So, like everyone knows, I was the only one there when he was sentenced. His mom's ex-boyfriend was there as well. But I was there... I kept on going. They put me in the newspapers all the time, used pictures of me without asking, but I could handle it because I've got God backing me up. I don't need an army of bikers. You see, with all my angels around me, it's not going to work. So I used to go into court and they used to say to me like, 'Oh, look, she's got make-up on, she's going to look for another man after the court case.' They used to say things like that and then they used to say to me, especially one woman, she screamed at me once, said to me, how pathetic I was, what a terrible mother I was. She used to insult me every time she went past me. I used to smile at her, because that's my personality. Instead of me wanting to go smash her face up, I would rather just pray. I would, like, forgive her, like Jesus said on the cross."

"You've picked a hard road," I told her. "And you may be very strong, but you can't tell me this hasn't hurt you."

"It has – of course it has," she said. "I even spoke to my mom once. My heart was very sore and I said to my mom, 'Why, after so long, when I decide to let my walls down, let my heart open, let someone in, why am I back to being alone? Why is it taken away from me?' It's like, they took him away from me, basically ... That's what they've done – they took him away. When I met him, I didn't want to let go of him. When he wanted to go home, I was like, 'No, just stay more. Don't go home.' I was like, so attached to him. So when he left, it was like a huge thing, because all of a sudden I was alone. So it's not about being single, it's not about having someone, it's about being with him."

Then, suddenly, she turned the tables. She asked me a question.

"Those boys, the ones from the court case ... Have you spoken to them?"

"Yes, I have."

"And do you believe their stories?"

"Yes, I do," I said, "I really do."

"I don't think they all told the truth. I really don't."

"Why not?" I asked.

She leant towards me. "Being a victim myself, a lot of things didn't make sense. The way that one behaved."

I know who she means. She means Ben.

"I mean, if you're a victim, and this is traumatising you so much, you won't be sitting in court laughing. Him and his parents were sitting there laughing at Collan. He was supposed to be a victim, wanting to commit suicide and not able to deal with life?"

"He did try to commit suicide," I said hotly. "And he wrote his matric from a psychiatric hospital."

"Yes, maybe, but he also sat in court smiling. I was a victim – you don't do that, okay. Even till today, when people speak about it, I'm not going to be laughing about it. He was very … The way he looked at me, this kid, the way he was looking at me in court, he was like, provoking me. There's no other word. He checked me on social media and then I went through his things. He's got a girlfriend and he's fine with life. If you are a victim of something … even depression or suicide, you're going to make it clear on social media because that's where you seek your attention. That's where people who are depressed do it. He didn't seem depressed at all."

"People deal with things differently though," I said. "You're very forthright and strong. Not everyone can survive what you went through. To be honest, I think you are more of a victim than you let on."

"Look, I sat in court and I was, like, some of the things were hectic to hear, I won't lie. It was. But being a victim myself, a lot of things didn't make sense."

"I heard a lot of people say that Collan replicated what was done to him," I said. "That he went through all of the same stuff, that he was also a victim."

She agreed with me.

"He is, most definitely. You should have heard the tone of his voice when he told me about this kid that drowned and told me they made them do that stuff as well. He says this kid drowned because they made them do things they didn't want to do. So, the way Collan spoke he most definitely was a victim. And he said to me, like, the way he was coaching, it's the way he was taught. Okay, I don't think the video incident – I'm not sure what happened there … Like, I heard everything in court, they spoke about it … I don't know where this boy's head was during this incident of the video, but put yourself in his shoes, okay, if this guy is touching you, in all these ways that you don't like, are you going to lie there and relax and let him do it, when you don't like it? You're not. You're going to talk about it. Yes, I understand it's boys, it's worse. But I had a gun against my head. And I spoke about it. I spoke about it. I spoke about it to save my friend. To save other girls. I risked my life saving other girls."

"Do you think Collan is sorry?" I was curious. And, truth be told, I really wanted the answer to be yes.

"Yes, of course he is! Collan admits being wrong, although he doesn't admit to all of what they're accusing him of. He says he has done wrong things. We spoke about it because I said to him, 'If you're molested, you don't go molesting other kids, you don't do that. I didn't do that.' And that's when things about his past came out. We've spoken about it, of what happened to him. Collan says now he can look back and see the right and wrong of the whole story. I think – he doesn't say it, it's just my personal opinion – but I think he still feels how unfair it all is, because why aren't those people being punished for what they did to him? Why isn't the school punishing the right people?"

It's a question I had been asking myself for months.

"How did you end up testifying?" I asked her. "Did they call you as a character witness?"

She shook her head. "No, I had to testify because of what happened with the social worker who came to interview Collan. Because of what she told us and then what happened."

"What did she tell you and then what happened?"

"She came to my house to interview Collan and we were all sitting together. She said to me, 'You two look so calm together.' She sat there and she came across like this supportive person. Then she just went and twisted everything we said and stabbed us in the back, basically. Because she was threatened. She told us, in my house, that she was threatened! That if she does not suggest a long sentence on her report, she will lose her job. She told that to me and Collan, and that's why I had to testify in court."

"That must have been really hard for you."

"It was. I didn't like the state prosecutor at all. She was attacking me on being a mother, which has got nothing to do with the case. She was attacking me as a person, which had nothing to do with the case. If I was such a terrible person, I would have done what his other girlfriends did and turned my back on him.

"Obviously it's a bit sensitive when me and him start talking about it because we've got limited time ... but sometimes I would phone him or he would phone me, because they've got tickey boxes in prison. The prison that he's now in, Kutama, is very good; it's a private prison. It's like an American prison. When he went into Sun City, he needed to pay his way for everything: pay for a bed, pay this, pay that – that used to cost me a lot. And I don't even have money for myself. His mom has helped ... financially. But I think supporting him financially is one thing, being emotionally involved is another.

146

"When he was in Sun City, I went to visit him every weekend. I used to stand there … They used to know me by name. The police there used to know me. Sometimes I didn't even have to stand in the queue. They just let me in. But now he's in the new prison and I just can't see him any more that often because he's now so far away.

"But, you know how many friends he's got in there? People who he started connecting with and started taking to church in prison. Collan's changing people's lives in jail. I think, if he did not meet me, he wouldn't have made it. Collan wouldn't have been here today. I can tell you that now – he wouldn't have. Because he wouldn't have known what to hold on to, he wouldn't have known what to do, he wouldn't have known about God. God's your hero, God's your everything. Even in court I said to him, 'You know what, just be strong. This is just a stepping stone. You're exactly where God wants you to be.' Look, I'm not even angry about his sentence, because he is exactly where God wants him to be. Of course my heart is sore, because I want him, obviously, to be by me, but it's not my will, it's God's will. He's been inside for two years this year. And when he comes out, he comes out, that is up to God. God can release that man tomorrow. God can do that. I feel sorry for the people who are holding these grudges against him. All those people who judged me for sticking with Collan are sinning more than what Collan sinned."

I had simply been listening to Jolene, trying not to interject. But I struggled with her last statement.

"What about the parents? Forgiveness of a man who molests your child …? I don't know if I could do that."

But she was resolute.

"When my grandmother was murdered and I stood in court, I walked up to that man who killed her, and I said to him, 'I forgive you.' While he was busy being sentenced, I said that. In my mind, I heard my grandmother laughing and I knew she was okay. So I walked up to that man … 'Louwrens, I forgive you,' I said. 'I know you said to me I'm next, but I still forgive you.'"

"He didn't say that to you!"

"Yes, he said that to me. Then I walked away. And I am more free with that forgiveness than what I would have been if I didn't forgive him."

This couldn't have been easy for Jolene. I read up later about what happened to Alice Farina, Jolene's beloved grandmother, in 2013. It was the most brutal of murders. She was only 66 and her 43-year-old deaf-mute lodger was found guilty of the murder. After hours of torture, he suffocated her, then bathed the body, redressed her in pyjamas and put her into the same bed he was found sitting next to the day after. At the trial, he had threatened her granddaughter, Jolene, who was nearly mad with grief. For her to forgive him was definitely not lip service. Some powerful internal stuff must have happened there.

"So I can tell you now," she said, "these people need to let go. I know it sounds easy, but they need to forgive. They need to let Collan go for them to be freed, especially the kids. I think the parents' egos have truly done more damage than what damage Collan did to the kids. That's my personal opinion. I think the kids who were there, they were brainwashed a lot, most definitely. I can hear the way the parents ... the one parent ... I don't know who she is, she said, 'Ja, he raped my child.' In court, she screamed blue murder at me. She said to me, 'He's a rapist! He raped my child.'"

Jolene sipped her lemon water.

"Look, I didn't go when the kids were testifying; I just went at the end of the trial, when the sentencing was happening. And even though I went for so short, they still tried to hurt me and scare me. That one woman from Parktown made sure she got my ex all worked up against me, and his family. Then he phoned his mom and they started getting things together to have my child taken away from me. So I was on the verge of losing my daughter because of that woman. They had no, no, no right whatsoever to interfere in my life. She had no right. She tried to turn my mother against me. But my mom knows Collan. It's not that I don't have sympathy for the victims and whatever they went through – it also affected me emotionally and broke my heart – but I didn't freak out with the case, like, oh, you're a rapist, you're this, all of this...

"And, also, if he was this extreme sex pest, why did he go with me to church instead of leading me to bed? Why didn't he try to jump me if he's this extremely obsessed with sex and all these things? I won't say nothing happened between the two of us; it did, I won't lie, obviously. We're both young; that's what youngsters do, and we were in a relationship. When I got home after meeting him that first night I woke my mom up about 3 am, saying, 'Mom, I met my husband!' So, ja, afterwards, I think I knew him like two months or something, before something even went that far. So, if he was this extreme person, this sex pest, like they call him, why would it have taken him that long? I mean ... he's got respect, he's got standards, he's got values."

"Is that what you love about him?"

"You know, he's such a sincere person; he's such a loving, kind person. I used to bully him. I bullied him! I used to wrestle him off the bed; then he's like, full of bruises all over the next day. I can be a very hard person. I'm Portuguese. I'm open and I'm soft and I'm loving, but I'm very persistent. So if he'd done something I didn't like, I put him in his place right there and then. He's younger than me as well, and he would apologise straight away. Collan is such a good person. I love him for that. I really love Collan for that. He is not what people say he is, he's not. We don't live for people's acceptance, we don't live for that, we live for God's acceptance. And it's the work of God that he's doing in prison ... These people are so disappointed."

"Tell me about that. What is he doing in prison?" I knew the church was still very present for Collan – I'd heard that before speaking to Jolene.

"Collan's working for God now. He's got the time to read the Bible, study the Bible, he's got time. I keep on saying I'm so jealous because he's overtaking me. I've been on this path for five years," she laughs. "When I get into a situation and he says, 'You know what ...' – he calls me 'my love' – he says, 'You know what, my love, God says this and this and this. The Bible says this and this.' And I'm like, 'Where did you read that? I missed that! Where did this come from?' I've got peace with what's going on now, because God's got him exactly where he wants him. Exactly. So it was God's will for me to meet him; it was God's will for me to save him. Whether it's God's will for me to still be with him, I don't know – time will tell. I'm not in a hurry. I won't say he's holding me back in any way by being in prison, because in the time that he's been in prison I have learned a lot. I've got a job, I'm getting back on my feet again, I'm sorting my life out, my kid went to Grade 1 this year.

"He still phones me every day."

"How was it for you when he was sentenced?" I asked.

"It was hard, very hard. I needed all my faith. And when he went to jail a lot of people hated me, even from his family; they said I was the worst girlfriend under the sun! I wouldn't allow anyone to see him without me. They said I was possessive and jealous, but it's got nothing to do with jealousy, it's got nothing to do with being possessive or whatever; it's got to do with how I'm not going to go through all of this and have somebody come in there with the wrong mentality and break him down. I'm not going to allow it. I've got no guarantee of when Collan comes out that I'm going to still be the girlfriend. I've got no guarantee whatsoever. So ... you know what a huge risk this is for me? This is, like, a huge risk."

I felt for Jolene, I really did. It was indeed a massive risk and there was so much riding on it. In 2018, Collan Rex was sentenced to 23 years of prison time. By the time he got out, she would be 50. Was anyone worth that? Especially a convicted serial child molester? Jolene thought so.

"I've put so much time in here, so much emotion in here. What if tomorrow he comes out and he walks away? I've got no guarantee that he's going to still be here. I know he loves me. I know he needs me. The day he was sentenced I thought so quickly to, like, just write my number on a piece of paper and give it to him. He said that piece of paper saved his life. I also wrote: 'This is just a passing phase. God is with you and I'm with you.' I said, 'I can't go in there with you now, but I'm still here, I'm not going anywhere, and I'll love you to the end.' That piece of paper saved his life. He said when he was sentenced that the first thing that went through his mind was to kill himself. Because we all know what happens in prison. We expected that he was going to be raped now, because prisoners, they will rape people who touch children. But nothing happened to him. Even up until now, nothing has happened to him. And it's not like he's got protection or whatever inside there – no one's protecting him. No one's looking out for him. Nobody, but God."

We were both quiet for a minute, both dealing with inner turmoil of entirely different natures. I felt reluctant affection for this dark-haired girl, so hard and so soft at the same time. It can't have been easy. It still couldn't be easy.

"I spoke to him and he will see you."

"What?"

I wasn't expecting that.

"You don't want to go home and think about it?"

"No." She was smiling.

"I prayed about it and asked God to show me what's right. And Collan will see you."

Wow.

"But," she said, not without me. Even when his mom visited him he would say to me, 'But, Jolene, you have to be there.' He doesn't see anyone without me."

"Guess we're road-tripping then," I said.

A roadtrip. With a stranger. To a prison. To see a child molester.

"Guess we are!"

She laughed.

Chapter 17
The Boy Who Went to Prison
Collan Rex

"Don't worry, you get used to it."
  Prison guard from Kutama Sinthumule Correctional Centre,
  Louis Trichardt

I've never been to prison. Not as an inmate, nor as a visitor. This was a first on all levels. It was also the first time I'd ever driven 400 kilometres to meet a man I'd never spoken to, with a woman with whom I had less than four hours' talk time on the clock.

We left before sunrise, Jolene and I. A long time before sunrise. My alarm generally goes off at 4:20am – which is, well, morning. For me, 2:45am felt like the middle of the night. But to visit Collan we had to leave Jolene's place by 4am, so that we could be outside the prison by 8:30am when visiting hours started.

"Don't judge me for not wearing make-up," she ordered as she opened the car door, struggling with her handbag and a bag of stuff for Collan. "I just can't face doing it right now."

"Well, if it helps," I offered, "I'm not wearing any make-up and I generally don't wear much anyway."

"Yes, but that's you," she said. "I go nowhere without it."

"I don't think you need much," I said. "You have lovely features."

She laughed.

"Thanks, but no thanks. When it gets light, I'll start working on my face."

We had to call and book the visit in advance. I didn't think you had to book to see a person in prison, probably because, if I had given it any thought, I'd have assumed that prisoners aren't really busy. It's not as though if you don't confirm a time, they might step out for a while. No one is going anywhere. But you do have to make an appointment, and you can only go on weekends and public holidays, and if you're coming from far away – as we were – you have to apply for an extended visit.

To book you need a prisoner number, a request from the prisoner and a time. You also get a list of dos and don'ts.

Tinyiko, in Bookings, was very kind to me on the phone. She patiently explained the dress code (no green, yellow or orange clothing – those are the colours the prisoners wear – and no strappy tops, short skirts or ripped jeans), the things I was allowed to bring in for the prisoner (tape deck, books, portable radio with no HDMI port) and the things I couldn't (no metal spray can, no food, all toiletries to be in plastic). She also listed what would be permitted in the visiting area: nothing under the sun except clothes and my ID. It was like learning a whole new kind of etiquette. I was so paranoid about getting it wrong, I begged her to repeat it over and over again.

"I'm so sorry, Tinyiko, it's my first time."

"Don't worry, my dear," she said patiently, "you get used to it."

I didn't want to get used to it.

Driving through sunrise and into the day, Jolene and I spoke about our lives and the things we have in common, particularly the love we have for our children. "If they had taken *Jessica from me I would have killed myself," she said matter-of-factly. "She is my life and my reason for everything. I didn't see my mom a lot when I was growing up; she was all over the place. When I had Jessie, I promised myself I would be there for her in a way no one ever was for me. I would do anything to protect her and she knows it."

I believed her.

Once again Jolene brought up the victim boys and the idea that people needed to forgive Collan in order to get on with their lives.

"The problem is this," I said. "These boys were shamed afterwards. Publicly. One was in a rugby match when another boy said, 'I hear you like jerking people off.' He almost threw the game. Another hasn't told his parents what really happened because his father is very homophobic and he's afraid he will think he's gay."

She was quiet then.

"Another says he still smells and tastes Rex when he wakes up."

She sat up dead straight.

"What does he mean, he can taste him?"

I shrugged.

"Maybe it's metaphorical, but I don't know."

"Collan never did that. Never." She was very angry. And perhaps a little worried? I wasn't sure.

"He touched their genitals and he wrestled with them and he took it too far. He never did ... *that*."

"I didn't say he did. I said that one boy feels him when he wakes up."

"No, you didn't." She was shaking her head. "You said he tastes him."

There was an uncomfortable pause. I was glad I was driving so I didn't have to meet her eye. I just kept staring straight ahead.

"You better ask him that," she said.

"What?" I wasn't expecting that.

She was staring out the front window, jaw set.

"When we get to the prison. You better ask him that. I want to know the truth."

"Don't you think he's told you the truth?"

She was determined.

"If he hasn't, he will. Collan won't lie to me."

"Will you still love him anyway?"

"Yes, I will," her answer came quickly. "But I still need to know the truth."

We were quiet for a long while after that.

We got to Kutama just after 8am. The day was already very warm. I said to Jolene that it didn't look like a prison from the road; it had a face-brick wall and there were no guards at the entrance.

"This is actually very nice," enthused Jolene as we drove in. "What beautiful views!"

"You think the prisoners can see the views?" I asked doubtfully.

"Trust me, it's much nicer than the other place he was at."

We drove about 100 metres down a paved road, and parked in the very well-signposted visitors' parking area. These signs were the first surreal elements of a day that was already promising to be rather bizarre.

"Does that sign really say I'm parking at my own risk?" I wondered, looking at what seemed to be the most incongruent instruction at a prison. Like any shopping centre, or townhouse complex, there was a sign telling me that I was parking at my own risk and that the prison would not be responsible for anything that might happen to my car while it was parked there. Surely this was the one place in the world I wouldn't be parking at my own risk? Who steals from a prison car park?

Jolene was busily applying her make-up but looked up.

"Ja, it's a bit weird," she offered.

I hadn't brought any valuables with me, but I wasn't wild about leaving what I had brought in the car. Did the sign mean there had been a robbery in the car park? If so, was this a common thing?

Jolene was ready.

"Come on," she said. "Let's go."

Under the porch, in front of the jail, there were several tables with seats attached; they looked a little like picnic tables. In the sunshine you could imagine eating lunch with friends, the mountains in the background. The view was beautiful if you squinted a bit so that the electric fence disappeared.

At one table a guard checked my ID against the visitors' request forms.

Satisfied that I was who I said I was, he directed me over to the next table, where another officer unpacked what Jolene had brought for Collan: toiletries, family photos and some documents he needed to register for a course. Everything was counted, checked and examined before it was repacked into clear plastic with Collan's name on it. Then Jolene was given a detailed receipt.

"What happens to that stuff?" I asked her.

"Well, they give it to him after the visit; the receipt is for him so he knows what's in the bag."

From as early on as I can remember, my brain has been hardwired to hysteria whenever I was in an unfamiliar or awkward situation. I felt a wave of it come over me as we bought food vouchers from a different officer (this one wearing a hygiene hairnet) and another one as we handed over money for Collan's prison account to Tinyiko, to whom I apologised again for being so needy on the phone.

"Ah, don't worry," she said again, "you get used to it."

"I know, sorry ... It's my first time."

I said that a lot. I said it at reception when I placed my credit card and phone in a locker and was handed a key in return. Jolene was less apologetic, probably because she had to take all the hairpins out of her hair and the hairband holding her ponytail, and she'd gone to a lot of trouble with her hair.

"Why do I have to take them out? What's anyone going to use these for?"

I kept quiet. I had some ideas. I've watched 22 seasons of *Law and Order*.

"I'm sorry, it's her first time," I offered.

Those went into the locker as well.

Then we went to the search area. There's one room for men and another for women. While we waited, Jolene threw her hair forward and created an elaborate updo using her own hair.

I was impressed.

"See? You didn't actually need all that other stuff."

She eyed me suspiciously.

"Are you making fun of me?"

"No, I'm really not," I said hotly. "I'm trying to keep myself distracted from the sheer weirdness of all of this ..."

She laughed.

"It is a bit weird, isn't it?"

The door opened and a woman wearing surgical gloves came out and looked at us.

"Which one of you wants to go first?"

Jolene jumped up. "I'll go first!" she said.

Surgical gloves. Images of *Prison Break* swam through my mind.

"Tell me how it goes," I offered weakly as Jolene headed off with the woman.

Two minutes later the door opened again and the same woman came out.

"You can also come in now," she said brightly.

Yay.

As it turned out, all I had to take off were my shoes. It was a very vigorous search, though – rather like those when you walk through the detectors at the airport carrying anything metal or wearing a watch and the machine goes off. Yeah, like those, but they are just window dressing compared to these. In prison, they're very much more thorough. The last time my breasts got that kind of attention was from a teenage boy I met at Catholic Youth Camp.

The guard found a receipt in my pocket for coffee we had bought during the drive.

"Do you need this?" she asked.

"Um, no, I guess not."

She tossed it in the bin.

"You can't take it in with you."

And again, "I'm sorry, it's my first time."

With the search over, we were herded into a holding area; it was like a little school hall and smelled like one too, a combination of wood, linoleum and disinfectant. There were plastic chairs set out in rows, all facing the same way. On all the walls were signs declaring that bullying and gangsterism were not permitted in the prison and any inmate who felt he was on the receiving end of either should report it to the guards. I had a strong urge to laugh. It reminded me of the signs they put up in classrooms where bullying isn't tolerated either, and if you feel you're on the receiving end of it you should tell the teacher. I wondered if inmates reported it more or less often than children.

"Collan Rex!"

Another guard appeared at the door.

"Who's here for Collan Rex?"

Jolene and I put our hands up like obedient children.

"Follow me," he said. We did.

Several locked doors (one opening on to an outdoor area from which, I couldn't help noticing, you had no view of the mountains) and some passageways later we arrived at the visiting area. It was like a giant school hall with lots of the same picnic tables. Jolene was nodding in approval.

"Sam, this is actually really nice."

"Really?" I said doubtfully, taking a seat at one of the tables. It seems rather ... well, prison-y to me."

"Oy!"

I jumped. One of the guards was pointing at me. "That seat is the prisoner's seat. You can sit anywhere at the table except there."

I opened my mouth to apologise, but Jolene got in first.

"She's sorry, it's her first time."

She started to laugh and then stopped. Suddenly her whole face softened and looked very beautiful and she smiled past me. I turned around, and there in the doorway, was Collan Rex.

He was shorter than I thought he would be, just a little taller than me. He had grown his hair longer since the trial, and it was pulled back into a hairband. He had a full beard, neatly trimmed, and was wearing bright green prison garb. He looked healthy and well, his eyes bright.

He gave Jolene a big hug. If I was sure of nothing else, I was sure of how much they loved each other. There was an intimacy between them I've only rarely seen. They sat, held hands and talked about people they knew and things that had been happening, moving from English to Afrikaans and back again. I sat quietly until they realised that I was watching them.

"Well, thank you for making the time to talk to me," I said.

"Thank you for coming to see me," he said.

Jolene laughed.

"Come, ask your questions!" she said.

And so for two hours, I did.

Collan was very easy to talk to. In fact, his very openness made me feel uncertain. I had to keep reminding myself he was not just Jolene's fiancée; he was serving time for 144 charges of sexual assault – of minors, at that. And yet, he seemed a child himself. Was he worried about what I was going to ask? He didn't seem to be.

"Has Jolene told you what I'm doing, about the book I'm writing?" I asked cautiously.

He nodded and looked grave. "She said you're writing a book about what happened at Parktown Boys'. About me and about the sexual assault stuff."

"And did she tell you that I thought I would be writing about the survivors of a monster, but in the end realised I was just writing about victims. Including you?"

"She told me that."

I wanted to be clear. I owed him that.

"I can't condone what you did," I said. "And I won't in the book either. But I do believe that as much as you were the perpetrator, you were also a victim, because it happened to you when you were there."

"Ja, it did," he nodded.

"And if that's true, then it means that, more than just the perpetrator, you are the evidence of a system gone wrong."

He shrugged and looked regretful.

"It was always like that though. When I heard about the boy who drowned, I thought, ja, sounds like the camp I went on in Grade 8."

"Did you go to the same place?" I asked.

"I don't know, maybe. But it's the same activities and stuff. We also built rafts."

In most of my conversations with the victim boys and with their parents, that Grade 8 camp is the origin of much of the fear and loathing that seem to make up the emotional roller coaster that is Grade 8. You're a Parktonian after the camp, but for the year after you're still just dogshit.

"I don't know if it was the same camp, but when I heard about Enock, it sounded the same. We also slept two nights in the chalets and then two nights on the ground near the river. It was very cold. And the night we slept at the river they woke us up at midnight and again at 3am and we had to do all sorts of PT like fitness and push-ups. The head boy at the time got very physical with one of the kids; he was trying to make him say 'Parktown Boys' High School' with a lot of spirit and the kid didn't have enough energy in his voice, so he pushed him so hard in the chest he actually fell over in the circle. The Grade 8s were quite small, you know, and the matrics were quite big and they were very scary."

I was reminded of when I was at school, and being in Grade 8, which back then was Standard 6, and thinking, you really did see the matrics as grown-ups. I was nervous of them; I felt like a child in comparison. I've noticed with boys, far more so than girls, that the physical differences between a 13-year-old and an 18-year-old are enormous. In those few years in between, their voices break, they grow hair where there wasn't any before. Shoulders and abs appear, puppy fat disappears, and the initial awkwardness of the early teens develops into an animal elegance of movement. You've only got to watch a first-team rugby game compared to a Grade 8 or 9 one, to see the men versus the boys. I could imagine a little Collan, fresh from IR Griffith, in a boarding school for the first time, catapulted into a brutal system in the same way all the boys he molested had been. So many surprises, and few of them good.

"Did you always want to go to Parktown?" I asked. "Or did someone choose the school for you?"

He shook his head. "I chose it. When I was applying to high schools I was still living in Ferndale with my mom; we looked at a few schools there but I didn't want to go to Ferndale High because I heard it was very rough."

His mom has said the same thing since.

"My grandfather, he said to try Helpmekaar and Monument, and I thought about that, but then I saw something about an Open Day at Parktown, and I went there. As soon as I was there, I fell in love with what it was and didn't apply for anywhere else and I was accepted."

"What did you love about it?" I think I already knew the answer – the same one I've heard from almost all the boys and the parents I have spoken to. Its tradition, its history, the very certainty of what is good and strong and true there. I'm reminded of my conversation with Ben, when he walked me to my car after our first conversation. Despite everything that happened to him, he still loved what the school stood for.

"The school was good. It was a place you could feel proud to wear your blazer, and a place of belonging. I loved it there."

So many of them did.

I told him about the school he loved. I told him what the boys I had interviewed said about being in Grade 8.

He nodded.

"Was it as bad for you when you were there? Better? Worse?"

He shrugged.

"Look, it was hard, but you get through it, you know."

A few weeks later we spoke on the phone and I asked him the same question. He had more to say that time.

"That's the thing, I spoke to my mom the other day about this, and apparently my gran said I was quite traumatised by it – I don't remember, but my gran said I was. I just remember it as being normal. To go from Grade 7, where you're top of the school, to Grade 8, where you're doing push-ups and being made to stand outside in the cold, to being beaten, that's a big shock. But then everyone else is doing those things and experiencing the same stuff so it must be fine. We even thought that when some of the matrics [from 2009] got suspended for beating kids and initiation and stuff. The others still made us run, they made us do PT until we dropped, those push-ups, holding push-up position for ages, we still had to do it."

I don't understand this at all. I simply couldn't fathom it. I talked it over with a friend who had been to an all-boys' school, and he was as appalled as I was over the amount of violence and how everything veered towards being sexual. This, he said, had never happened at his school.

"But the matric/Grade 8 thing, that's tradition. You'll never stamp that out. It's part of the rite of passage."

"It's rite of passage for a child to be forced onto his knees by a matric who wants a hand job? And then be forced to eat polish if he won't?" I enquired hotly.

"No, of course not, but it's tradition to warm toilet seats for the Sixth Form and do push-ups and sleep outside on camp and stuff. It bonds them."

I went to a Catholic girls' school. The only thing I ever bonded to was the bus schedule for when I could go home. Some grades – back then we called them standards – were pretty good, some were pretty bitchy. I remember Standard 9 as being a particularly unpleasant year. But compared to what I was hearing … it seems I got an easy ride.

"You can't understand, Sam," my friend told me. "You didn't go to a boys' school and you're not a boy."

"So it's okay for this to happen to boys?"

He gave me a look that said, I am trying to talk to you across a continent of non-understanding.

"No. And yes. Sort of. You'll never get it."

Someone else said that the Grade 8 rite of passage is the same sort of thing as becoming a Navy Seal.

"They learn discipline and brotherhood. Those are the bonds that last a lifetime."

I don't see that the Grade 8 rite of passage is anything like becoming a Navy Seal. People who apply to become Navy Seals have a very good idea of what they will be up against. They know beforehand how tough the conditions are and they apply anyway. And, yes, there is sleep deprivation and push-ups forever (although I'd been informed by some of the boys they were made to do 80 push-ups at a time and that's 30 more than the average Seal hopeful has to be able to do in two minutes), but these people are already fully trained soldiers before they enter the programme. And they get to opt out at any point. These children have no choice, and "children" is the operative word.

Conscription came up as well ... Men my age and older, talking about how the army taught them discipline and respect. Fear makes the best followers – that echoed in my ears from my conversation with Seth.

The hostel test came up with every boy. On the face of it, it seemed simple. The Grade 8s had to know everything there was to know about Druce Hall and its history, everything about the matrics, including all their accomplishments, their full names and all they'd ever achieved on the sports field. Passing the hostel test relied largely on how the old pots felt about the new pots at the time. On a genial day, the questions might be as easy as naming the prefects in the boarding house. On a tough day, boys would be expected to know every important date in the school's history and the CV of every prefect. And even if you got it all right, there was no guarantee of a pass. That was given at the discretion of the matrics in the room at the time of the test. Several boys who got all the answers right were failed because of their "attitude", especially true of one in particular who was regularly accused of thinking he was better than he was because he didn't participate enough in hostel sports. A fail meant punishment, and the severity of that was decided by the matrics. Collan himself had not escaped pain for failing the hostel test. He remembered it well.

"The one time when I failed my hostel test, the matrics made us do push-ups on the bottom field and the one said I wasn't doing the push-ups correctly so he kicked me in my ribs and hit me and knocked my head on the ground. My nose was bleeding, but he made us run again and again. It didn't matter."

"Did you at any point think to yourself, this is really screwed up? Did you talk it over with the other Grade 8s?"

He shook his head.

"Now I realise it was like brainwashing by the culture and system. They want you to be part of it and not try to change it. It's the whole 'If you cry, you die' thing. Taking everything they throw at you is how you become a man. You're a boy when you enter Parktown; Grade 8 is the year you start becoming a man."

"Do you think the teachers knew what was going on?" I asked.

He laughed.

"Those Old Boys, they knew about the initiations and the goings-on. They knew. Look, there was stuff they might not have known … I mean, when I was living there, I didn't know what the matrics were doing to the Grade 8s in terms of the sexual stuff, making the kids give blow jobs and that. I was living there and I didn't know, so maybe they didn't know that stuff, but in terms of the beatings and the initiations, they knew."

This was what Collan revealed to me on the phone sometime later, but back at the time of my visit to the prison I asked him about the sexual initiations he had been through. I trod carefully, but he was very open about it.

"Throughout high school, kids used to hit each other in the balls and stuff. All the older boys were very physical with us. Even the teachers used to hit us with various objects like hockey sticks; one teacher made us do knuckle push-ups on pencils while our feet were up on top of the heater. Thing is, you thought it was innocent, but actually you never knew what people's intentions actually were. Sometimes a guy would come up to you and make like he was going to fight you and then he would tap your genitals – that's the kind of thing that was going on."

"And was that in Grade 8 or did it continue?" I asked.

"It never stopped throughout school, the sexual stuff. Even when you're in Grade 9, there's a Grade 10, or in Grade 10, there's a Grade 11. It doesn't have to be the matrics. Anyone is allowed to have physical dominance over you. There were times when I was very uncomfortable with a boy in the grade above me; I mean, I liked him, but he made me uncomfortable. In prep he used to make me sit next to him, and I would try to get away from him. He played 'Man or Mouse' with me; some of my own peers also played that. The other guy's hand is near your crotch and if you say 'Mouse' he will move his hand down your leg towards your knee and if you say 'Man', he will grab and squeeze your genitals and then you know you're a man. It never stops."

I asked him about waterpolo. Collan was very athletic at school. Jolene said that if I were to go to his grandfather's house I would see that there were medals everywhere that Collan had won, for athletics and rugby, but mainly for waterpolo. His whole face came alive. Waterpolo was his passion.

"In Grade 8, I tried everything. It was my first time playing rugby and I loved that; I was in the B team, so I wasn't the best at it. Everyone encouraged me to try out for waterpolo because it's very physical and really good for fitness, especially if you're playing rugby. I'm a very physical person, and they said I was very strong. So then I tried waterpolo and made the A team. I played and played and I loved it. I made the Gauteng under-16 A team. The first tournament we played we came second and I got a medal."

Again, we would talk more about waterpolo on the phone a few weeks later, because waterpolo had not been a simple game, even back then. In fact, back then was when all the problems started.

"Even in waterpolo, they would grab you down there or even outside of the water, they would try to hit you down there. I remember, for our first team waterpolo fines evening, the whole team got together and for every fine you got, you had to drink. So they got all of us juniors drunk and we all passed out. In the morning, one of my friends told me that one of the matrics had curled up next to him and tried to grab his balls and stuff and touch him."

"And that wasn't scary for you?" I asked.

"It was just part of it," he said.

Just part of it.

"In matric, I had a chance to go to the States. There was a scout from Lindenwood University. I just went to recruiting websites and he saw me play in videos," he said wistfully. "They offered me a 75 percent scholarship to go and play there. He spoke to my coach and so did I, but when it came down to the money, my grandparents couldn't afford it. So I couldn't go."

I wondered how things would have been different if he had.

"You know, sport made me happy. I think I was the happiest when I was in school. We were the great waterpolo team then, we even beat KES."

"And it never occurred to you that what was happening to you was wrong? It never crossed your mind that older boys were molesting you and it wasn't okay?"

"No," he said, "it was just how it was."

The same question would come up in court later though.

Jolene had waited long enough.

"Ask him. Ask him that question."

I was thrown. We were still talking generally about Collan's own schooling, and I wasn't ready to go in with *that* question. But Jolene was. Collan looked confused.

"What question?"

"Maybe we can get to it later," I offered weakly, but Jolene was having none of it.

"Tell him what you told me in the car."

I looked at Collan. He was curious and alert, his eyes fixed on mine, his hand holding Jolene's.

"Well, I was telling Jolene in the car about some of the boys, and how they haven't got over what happened to them. Not just with you, but with the experiences they had with their matrics and the initiations."

Collan looked upset.

"What do you mean they haven't got over it?"

"I mean a lot of them are still sad, Collan. One wrote matric from a psychiatric hospital. More than one attempted suicide. Their marks are bad. Some are on medication."

Ben especially had struggled more than he had let on.

"Most of the time I was happy about what I did," Ben had said. "But a lot of the time I was just thinking I wish he never existed and then nothing could have gone wrong. I felt lost. All the time. And at one point I got upset and felt like I didn't want to live any more ... My dad and my brother were in the car and I just hopped out and I ran for like apparently an hour long. I came to a bridge over the N1 and I just decided to hang there and I thought, I'm just going to jump. Basically, while I was hanging there, I was hanging by one arm ... Ja, I just held with one arm and I felt like I wanted to fall, and at the time I wished I had. But the one thing that kept me back was seeing this, which is my family. And I didn't want to disappoint people. It goes through my mind still. You're going to live or you're going to die, so you're wasting your time here anyway. There's no point in doing anything because again, it's got to come to an end. I don't believe in anything after death because it just makes no sense to me. Just to think, it's all gone, nothing's left. If you die, there's nothing left. It doesn't make any difference to anybody else, you are yourself ..."

I could think of a lot of people to whom it would have made a difference. And it was after that that the Archivist sent him to a psychiatric hospital.

"I enjoyed Beethoven. Maybe because I got to ... mainly because I got to chill. I think the main reason I enjoyed it was simply because I actually got along with people. People had their own problems, and it was cool because as soon as you start to listen to people, you get along very well. But physically and mentally I wasn't feeling great. I kept on telling the doctor that I wasn't sleeping well ... or that I didn't have enough energy for the day; eventually I was taking 26 tablets a day. I wrote all my exams from there. I know I wrote at a school, I remember where, but I don't remember anything else. I don't remember getting a lift there, I don't remember which exam I wrote each day. I told my parents I was studying very hard and ... maybe in my head I was, but I know I didn't actually study a single thing. Besides history because I ... liked history, but I don't know how much I remembered."

When I related this to Collan he looked devastated. He put his hand up to his mouth.

"I don't want them to be sad. I'm sorry I hurt them."

He really did look sorry.

Jolene pressed on.

"Tell him!"

"One boy said he can still feel you and taste you ..." I hated saying it. I hated thinking it.

Jolene turned to face Collan; they had been sitting next to each other, heads together, but now she drew back.

"You need to tell me right now. Why does he say that?"

Collan looked at her.

"I don't know why he would say that."

"You need to tell me right now. When you touched those boys' genitals, was it because you wanted to be dominant over them or was it because you are sexually attracted to boys?"

His eyelids flickered. When my son does that, I know he's telling a lie. When my husband does that, it's because he's stressed. I couldn't tell here.

"No, I never did that. I never – and I never tried to make anyone else do that. I never."

He looked at me.

"She says she will love you no matter what your answer," I offered.

It was all I had.

"I never did that."

"What did you do?" I asked.

"Like I said in court, I touched them where I shouldn't have. Sometimes I wondered why I crossed the line like that. I remember now and then, like when I choked Ben until he passed out, that gave me a real big fright. That was a big scare, and I thought, why am I doing that, why am I crossing that line? Another boy passed out as well. When I grabbed their genitals, it was like, I don't know how to explain, for me to get dominance over them; I felt like I was the stronger one, that I was the one with power. That's how it got to me always grabbing them. And I felt bad sometimes when I knew I had hurt them, when they expressed they were in pain."

"Did you ever say sorry to any of them?" I asked.

"I wanted to," he said vigorously. "I really did. I wrote a long letter to be read out at my sentencing where I apologised for hurting them but my lawyer wouldn't let me read it; he said it would make me look more guilty."

"And afterwards?"

"Afterwards I was in prison."

"I'm an alcoholic," I said, "and one of the things you're supposed to do as part of the 12 steps of recovery is to make a list of anyone you've harmed and, where possible – where to do so wouldn't cause greater damage – to try to make amends."

He nodded.

"Is that something that ever goes through your mind?"

"Of course it does," he said. "I did feel remorse. Because of my bail conditions, I wasn't allowed to contact any one of the boys or anyone at Parktown, so for me to tell them I was sorry was difficult, and when the judge said to me I hadn't shown remorse, I was like, well, how can I? I told them in court I didn't mean to hurt them; I didn't want to hurt any of them. With all those attempted murder charges, I said in court I didn't mean to kill them or hurt them. I didn't ever want to hurt them. I didn't."

He leaned forward. "Have you spoken to *Tyler?" he asked.

"No, not yet," I said.

I'd spoken to Tyler's mother months before, but she was very cautious. Tyler had struggled terribly with what had happened to him at Collan's hands. He had stopped playing waterpolo.

"If Tyler was sitting here now in front of you, what would you say to him?" I asked.

"If I could speak to Tyler now? I hope he could forgive me and that one day he could find healing and this doesn't overwhelm his life. All those boys saw me as their friend and I hurt them; the way I've impacted their lives caused a ripple effect and I know that. After I got arrested I met one of the boys from the waterpolo club and he told me that some of the victim boys were taking drugs and fighting and getting out of hand. And I didn't want that to happen to their lives."

Later he would talk more about this on the phone. "I am sorry for hurting them. I don't want their futures to be affected. I actually really wanted them to prosper in waterpolo. Some of them were really good players. I wanted them to do well. And I'm the one who probably took their love for that sport away, or even hurt them to the point they don't want to play any more, so that hurts, because I know how it feels. Because my passion was waterpolo, coaching, refereeing, playing, all of it ... Now I can't do that any more. So I understand I took away a passion of theirs and I never wanted to hurt anyone in that way."

I believe that. I believe him.

"I wanted to get out of Parktown," he said. "I felt myself becoming more angry and more irritable. I actually applied for the job of water-polo coach at two other schools, St Stithians and St Benedict's. The week before I was arrested, I went to St Benedict's for an interview. I just wanted to be out of Parktown; I felt like, if I could go somewhere else, I could start again and everything would be better."

On the phone, he discussed many times his last weekend before the arrest. He's played it over and over in his mind. It was the first time he had ever lost his temper in a game.

"It happened on a Saturday. The team went to Affies for a match in the morning; we played against them and my team lost. I felt like I was becoming like my old coach and being angry and aggressive and I wasn't normally like that. We did lose badly, but I calmed down and then me and some of the boys went back to the school and hung around in the common area and, yes, then the whole wrestling thing happened with Jonah and some of the others. Then we all went to Zoo Lake to play a friendly. I felt like the ref wasn't playing with a full house and he red-carded me. It was the first time I acted out on a ref's decision. I threw the ball at him, and I stormed out of the pool. I walked past aggressively, but I didn't threaten him or hit him. I can't remember what I said to him. Then that Thursday I got arrested. I came out of jail the following week on the Monday and on Tuesday St Benedict's let me know I had the job. I had to let them know I couldn't take it."

I could feel his sadness. Did he really think everything would be different? Could it have been?

Back at the prison, we talked more about his life outside of Parktown.

"I lived with my mom mostly," he said. "My dad and her were separated and he then died when I was quite young. I don't remember much about him. My ouma told me we were close. When I was four years old my mom got married and had my sister, and then about eight years later my mom got a boyfriend who lived with us. He was quite verbally abusive towards me and I had to see a psychologist about it for quite a while.

"My mom was away a lot of the time. At one time, I didn't see her for about a year and a half. Then she came back and she was pregnant with my brother; he's much younger than me. I was in Parktown by then and things were okay. I used to go home to my ouma and oupa on weekends. I loved my ouma so much. She got cancer when I was in Grade 8 but she wanted to see me get to matric and she did, although she passed away that year. To say she was the glue of the family is not enough here; she protected me, she kept everyone going, she was someone you could trust. She was such a tiny person but so much strength and so much wisdom. She was the only one pushing church and pushing God in my life. She wanted me to embrace God and now I see why.

"When I left Parktown after matric, I went to Varsity College to study sports management and development; it was a diploma course, and at the same time I was coaching waterpolo at Parktown as an assistant coach and I was still living with my grandfather. I moved into the hostel in 2015. I was playing club waterpolo with some of the masters who were already there. It was great."

I chose not to ask Collan about the night of his arrest during that prison visit. I'd already thrown an awful lot at him and he was looking tired.

"Shall I leave you two alone?" I offered. They both looked confused.

"Why?" asked Jolene.

"So you can have time to be together without me," I offered. "Wouldn't you like that?"

They looked at each other and Collan shrugged. "Don't you have more things you want to know?"

"Well, yes, but aren't you tired?"

"I'm hungry," he said, smiling. "Can I get anything for you ladies?"

When he went to fetch food from the concession stand, I hissed at Jolene.

"Don't you want to be alone with him?"

"No, it's fine. I'm also listening!"

I felt uncomfortable. They hadn't seen each other in months and I felt awkward sitting in on what was essentially their time together.

"I'm going to the bathroom. When he gets back you need to talk to him about how long he would like to be alone with you!"

Alone was perhaps a poor choice of words. There were now a lot of prisoners and their families and friends in the visiting hall. All the prisoners were wearing yellow, green or orange, in very bright hues. They looked harmless, like helpers at a trampoline place or an obstacle course. I had to keep reminding myself that this was a maximum-security prison and no one was in here for jay-walking or loitering.

Collan came back bearing food and cold drinks.

"Collan," I said, "I'm going to the bathroom so you and Jolene can talk."

They exchanged glances.

And then I left. They search you every time you come out of the bathroom. I went three times.

When I got back there was a naartjie-flavoured mineral water on the table. Both of them were smiling. Collan said, "We've decided you can leave, but you have to drink the water first and take very small sips."

Didn't they want to be alone, I wondered? Or were they just being super polite?

"Tell me about the night you were arrested," I asked.

"I didn't know the cops were there. I knew Jonah's mom was there and he was worried too. He kept saying he didn't know why his mom was there. He was stressing, saying what did he do now, why was he in trouble, and I told him I'd try to find out. I went to see Mariolette and she told me that they were just having a meeting so I went back down to the hostel and I told Jonah there was nothing to worry about. I went back to my room. Then Mr Bossert came and said, 'Bring whatever you need, and put long pants on and let's go.' And then he told me they were arresting me, what they'd seen on the cameras, me touching Jonah. I went to the police van and they didn't handcuff me. They said they didn't think I would run away, so I climbed in the back. Then I messaged Jonah to say, 'Your mom was here for me', and he messaged back, 'I know, it's so fucked up. I know you were just joking.' I actually wanted to use that in court, but my lawyer said I shouldn't.

"I was arrested on the Thursday night, and obviously they don't

168

charge you immediately. Anyway, that entire weekend I was in Hillbrow Police Station. I came out on the Monday and the judge dropped the charges temporarily, pending further evidence. Then my mom came to pick me up and we came straight back to Roo-depoort. All my stuff had already been removed from my room and was already there. When I told my oupa, he thought the whole thing was ridiculous and my mom, she didn't say much; she was just there for me. She kept saying, 'Don't worry, it's going to be okay' and stuff."

But it wasn't, I thought. It would never be okay again.

"At that time, did you know what the charges were going to be?" I prodded. "Or that there would be as many as there were?"

"No. It happened so weirdly. The first time I was in court that Monday, it was eight charges. Then, when I came back a week and a half later, it was 15 charges, then 27 charges; I mean, it just kept on growing. At one stage it went from 37 to 87 and then to 160-something. It didn't stop until they eventually submitted the indictment. At that point I had a private lawyer; every time I went into court I paid him R1000 and that was out of my own pocket. He said we were going to plead not guilty and that everything was going to be okay and we would prove it by telling how these things were done to me. I would tell what happened to me and give names of who did stuff to me, and that was, I guess you could call it the game plan. And also, at the time I was doing it, I was young – 18,19, 20. But I couldn't afford [the lawyer] for very long, so I had to use the public defence lawyer, who wasn't very good."

"You pleaded guilty to 144 charges," I began, but he was already shaking his head vigorously.

"No, I never pleaded guilty," he said firmly. "I pleaded not guilty with admissions."

"Why did you admit to all of those charges though? Surely you could see that that wasn't going to end well for you?"

He agreed.

"For my bail application, my lawyer told me to put what I thought people might say I had done. And then my other lawyer said I must just write down those same things for all the different boys. And I thought that was for a plea bargain because the second lawyer said that was my only hope. So I just ticked off what I thought they thought I'd done."

"Was there a plea bargain?" I asked.

"No, but I only found that out when I heard I was still facing, like, 187 more charges!"

"Were you shocked at the sentence?"

I've often wondered about this – Collan's reaction to the sentences passed down – because I don't see how he could expect much less time for the number of offences of which he was found guilty.

Both nodded their heads.

Jolene spoke first.

"When the social worker came to see us, she said she wanted to recommend a suspended sentence or a hospital stay or something like that because she could see Collan had had it done to him. But she told us that she had been told that if she did that, she would lose her job, so we knew he would get jail time. But we were thinking a few years or probation. We never saw 23 years."

"Did she really say that?" Are social workers allowed to say things like that? It seemed really dubious to me. And, from the outside, I battled to understand how neither of these two could see how that there was no chance a judge could be seen to be minimising this.

"She really did," Jolene said. "She was very nice, because she under-stood those things were done to Collan."

That was highlighted in her sentencing report. The Archivist sent me a copy. This is what she writes on page six:

"The accused informed that through his years in school and in the hostel, he was exposed to bully, wrestling and games which involved the touching of genitals. It was an accepted norm among learners to grab, hit or touch each other's genitals with the aim of proving one was not fearful of the other. Moreover, games such as 'man or mouse' were played in which a learner would place their hand near the other person's genital area and ask the question, 'Are you a man or mouse?' The response would generally be, 'I am a man', thus lead-ing to the learner moving their hands towards the genitals, eventu-ally ending up grabbing the genitals. According to the accused, the purpose of the game was to prove that one was a man who did not have any fears."

And this is on page seven:

"The accused ... recalls that even at their waterpolo practice ses-sions, their coach would encourage touching of each other's genitals as this was explained as a strategy to gain power over your opponent. The accused felt he adopted and practised his former coaches' style of training and teaching on the victims."

"Why wouldn't you give names in court?" I asked Collan.

He looked sad.

"No one asked me properly in court who did those things to me. In court the judge asked me if the same things were done to me and I said yes. I told the story of my school coach who made all of us stand in the pool and then pulled my penis out as far as he could and let go. It was so sore I actually jumped in the air. He did it to all of us. Then the judge asked me if it was like initiation things and I said ja, but they were general questions; they never asked for specifics of people to put the blame on for that."

I knew this wasn't true and I told him so.

"Luke Lamprecht did ask for specifics in court and you wouldn't tell him," I said.

"No, he didn't. Nobody did." Collan was upset.

"Collan, he did. Two separate people remember it. When your lawyer was cross-examining him on the stand and said to him that the same things had been done to you, he said that if you gave him names, he would go after them as hard as he went after you."

He was shaking his head.

"I don't remember that at all."

"I promise. And those people have no reason to lie."

He was silent.

"Do you think you might have blocked it out?"

He nodded.

"Some days when I sat there, I didn't hear anything – especially after I was found guilty. Sometimes I felt like I wasn't there."

I wouldn't let it go.

"Collan, did people do things to you that you then did to these boys? Did they?"

"Yes, they did."

"So you're in prison for what could be the rest of your life and they are walking around outside and that's just fine?"

"Obviously, it's not just fine, but I guess I've got to a stage where I've forgiven everyone. For me now to go and chase them, to damage reputations … Some are married with children. I understand I'm here for 23 years, but some have a lot to lose. And it's a huge snowball effect."

"You lost your life," I said. "You will be in prison for as long as you had been alive when you were sentenced."

He was quiet.

"Do you ever feel like you've been hung out to dry? Like it was easy to blame all the bad stuff on you?"

"Yes, but that's life and it happens. It's in the past."

I left it. And changed the subject.

"Tell me about Jolene," I said. Collan lit up. Jolene blushed and stood up to go to the bathroom.

"Ah, Jolene," he smiled. "I wanted to take her out the day after I met her in a club. I asked her if I could go visit, but she said she was going to church and I was like, church? Agh, you know ... It was only later that I realised how important it was to her, and how important it would become for me.

"The more I got to know her, the more she realised who I was as a person, and the more I was in love with her. I was so scared to tell her who I was. I remember the first time I told her was in my car. I said, 'I'm on trial and this is what for,' and she was very quiet for a minute. I didn't know if I should leave or if she wanted me to stay. And I told her I would leave if she told me to, but she didn't and she gave me a hug. I was confused because for anyone, it would be logical to run away once I told her, but she didn't run. We started having such a connection. Being with her, it felt right to me. And she decided no more drinking, no more going out; so we started relaxing and getting to know each other, which was really amazing. I got to know her past and I got to be the one she could talk to. And I realised how she was put on in the past, but she is so loving and caring. She cares about people in the most amazing way – you wouldn't even think of doing things for others the way she does, but she just goes and does it.

"We are engaged and all I want is to get out and be a good husband to her. When I was still in Sun City, we wrote letters to each other. We both had a book we wrote in; she had one and I would have one, and we would exchange them every week. It's how we kept the love alive. And if she had a blue day, she'd write to me. She'd tell me she loved me and was missing me. And that would make me feel better because I loved her and I was missing her."

Jolene returned and took her seat.

"You guys done?"

Collan was grinning broadly and, all of a sudden, so was I.

"With that, yes." I said.

"You'd better tell me everything he said when we're in the car," she laughed.

"I hope I remember it all," I said innocently.

"Ja, well, you better!"

"A couple of people told me you were moved from Sun City because you were very badly beaten," I said to Collan.

He shook his head.

"I was never harmed at Sun City, not once."

"Although I bet some people would be sad if they knew that," Jolene said cynically.

"You must have been scared though," I said.

"But, Sam, I was so scared when I found out I was going there. It was quite hectic. I was dressed in a suit the day I was sentenced but then, because of all those bikers ... It was too dangerous for me to go out the courthouse. The bikers said they would fuck me up, so they took me straight into the cells and, because I was in a suit, all the other inmates thought I was a lawyer. The shock just, like, hit me; I was so tired, I didn't know whether to cry or sleep. The few hours I was there I was thinking, what now, what now? And then the transport came to Sun City and suddenly I was going to jail."

In future phone conversations, Collan would describe to me what it was like.

"First night, you sleep on a mattress on the floor and then you get assigned to a section. They were going to send me to a section where there were a lot of people on the floor so I had to pay one guy to keep me safe, which was quite hectic.

"You pay for a lot of things: you pay for a nice towel, you pay for extra food, you pay for a lot there. And everyone knew me because I had been on the news the whole time, but I didn't know anyone. I was scared. I didn't know where to go or who to speak to. One person was trying to give me this advice and another person as well, and I didn't know if they were gangsters or not so ... Yes, it was quite hectic. I was afraid I was going to have to join a gang just to be safe. In fact, before I got sentenced, I had some friends who knew the system and were in a gang. I even asked them if I should join the 7s, so inside the prison I would at least be okay, and be accepted. But it turns out that if you don't bother them, they don't bother you. And luckily I found the Church almost immediately.

"I didn't think about church at first, but then this one guy who I made friends with invited me, so I went there. He introduced me to the senior pastor, who talked to me and invited me to get involved. They started looking out for me and helping me when I needed things, and created a family. And you can see in a person if someone is genuine or not. This guy, some days we would just sit and eat; he'd make a sandwich or open a packet of chips and talk about God, and everything.

"That really helped to take my mind off stuff.

"I did get depressed there. Sometimes I had to climb under my blanket for the day because I didn't want to get up; I didn't want to go anywhere ... I had started teaching English, but sometimes I would tell them, 'No, I can't do it today, I'm not sleeping well', and I'd just sleep all the way through."

I asked Collan if it was any better where he was now.

"Much better. Here at Kutama, I've registered for some classes because I want to study, and I've joined some of the sports teams and games clubs – and church on Sunday, obviously. I also joined a health awareness group because HIV levels are crazy so we try to get awareness going within the prison. I keep quite busy.

"I also get down sometimes. Talking to family really helps, but there are times when you can't because we're locked down from 5:30pm so if you want to talk to family later, that's hard – that's very hard. During hard times I need to keep my mind busy and read. I mostly read things about the Word of God. Either from the Bible or something about the Bible to help me get my mind off what's bothering me. There are times where you feel there is too much sadness."

I asked whether he ever thought about going back to Parktown.

"I think about it all the time in prison. I know what I want to say, something along the lines of where I apologise, but also motivate people to arise beyond what the expectations of Parktown are and what the culture of Parktown is. To tell those boys to stand up for what they believe – don't let anyone crush those dreams of theirs. I want to motivate them and say sorry for what I did, but also say: let not the Parktown culture awaken again, let it be rooted out so we can all 'Arise' above it. I've been reading the scriptures a lot and there are some Bible verses in Jeremiah, actually Jeremiah 31:6, with the word 'arise' in them that got me to thinking."

He gave me the verse: "For there shall be a day that the watchmen upon the mount Ephraim shall cry, Arise ye, and let us go up to Zion unto the Lord our God."

"It's about how in times of trouble, when you feel you've lost everything, that's the time to stand up, and you go to God, so you arise from your pain and from your loss."

Three hours went very quickly. Before we ended the visit, Collan and Jolene hugged. He turned to me, but I put my hand out to shake his. I couldn't hug him. Even though my instinct was to do exactly that.

By the time we left the prison, Jolene was tired.

"Go to sleep," I said. "I'll wake you when we stop for food."

"No, I'll feel bad if I don't stay awake with you," she said. But I could see she was utterly drained.

"I will wake you up if I start getting sleepy," I promised.

I wanted her to sleep. I was completely thrown by my own feelings. I still believed Collan belonged in prison. I still believed that he knew what he had done was wrong. But ...

He seemed so child-like, so unable to comprehend the full damage of his actions. He was little more than a child himself. He had come through a difficult and complicated childhood; he had himself been abused at school, and taught that it was all perfectly normal behaviour. And so he had continued the horrific tradition that he himself had learned. He had been a "man" instead of a "mouse". And look where it had got him. I went to interview a monster, but all I found was a man.

Chapter 18
The Boy Who Was an Angel
Petro

I really wanted to talk to Collan's mother, Petro. That he adored her was clear; his face lit up at the prison when I asked whether he would ask her to talk to me.

"I want to get a picture of you growing up," I said. I knew his father had passed away when he was young, and his beloved ouma had died of cancer while he was in matric.

"She will speak to you," he said confidently. Not the first time I was astounded at the trust people put in me to tell their stories. The pressure woke me up sometimes at night and I prayed very hard about it, that I would do everyone justice, and that their voices would be heard.

Petro had been something of an enigma. She'd seldom been seen in court, but had kept up with what was happening there, first from reports and then from Jolene, who was there for every day of the sentencing.

When Jolene sent me Petro's number, her WhatsApp picture struck me. She was young and very pretty, and Jolene bore a striking resemblance to her, although I didn't say that to either of them. She had long dark hair, wonderful bone structure and the same eyes as her son. When I called her, she was sweet and eager to talk about her beloved boy.

"From the day he was born, Collan was such a honey. My mom used to ask him, 'Where do you hide your wings?' He was such an angel, such a cheerful child. He was open and loving – he is still the apple of my eye. I never had problems with him, never ever. He was bullied at school, so it was a bit hard on him, but nothing else unusual.

"His father died of a heart attack at 32, when Collan was 11, and it was very sad. By the time Collan was two, we were already separated.

I didn't want Collan to be between two houses as a little boy, so I kept him with me as much as I could. I wanted him to have a stable home with me and my then husband who loved Collan very much – he still does. But at that stage he was drinking very heavily, so I said to Collan that maybe he should live with his dad for a while, but then his dad passed away. Collan was still a child. I felt so bad for him, but he just said to me, 'Don't worry, Mommy, I understand.'

"Although he and my ex are good friends now, when my ex was drinking, it was bad. My son used to stand up to his stepdad for his sister, to protect her from him. My ex was never violent with the children, but he would want to drive them in the car when he had been drinking. Collan didn't want him to drive with his younger sister; he would stop him from putting her inside. There's a four-year age difference between them, and he practically raised her. I was working long hours at that stage, so he would make her food, wash their clothes in the afternoon when they got home from school. Like I said, he was such a honey.

"He used to worry about me a lot because of the abusive relationship I was in. He would come to my rescue, that kind of thing. It was never physical – my ex never hit me – but it was verbally abusive. Collan didn't get along with my ex-husband until he went to rehab and got clean, and things are much better now.

"When Collan went to Parktown, he was staying with my mom. I was in a space where I couldn't afford to put him in that school. We were staying in Ferndale at the time and we looked at Ferndale High, but it didn't have a good reputation back then; we heard stories about drugs being taken there. Parktown seemed a much better option. But I'll never forget seeing him the first time after orientation. He was like a scared little rabbit. I don't know what happened there. He never really spoke about it to me, but I know some abuse went on at the camp. There was even stuff in the newspapers about it. I don't know exactly what they did to the kids there. I think he's blocked it out.

"He didn't tell me anything for a long time. But he did tell me that when he started playing waterpolo, he got grabbed in the water and that they used to sharpen their toenails in waterpolo so they could cut the boys in the water. That's how he was coached, so that's the kind of coach that he became. It's like monkey see, monkey do.

"He never told me about the sexual stuff that happened to him at school. He told his grandfather later, before the trial, what had happened, but they had this saying there, 'What happens at Parktown stays at Parktown', so I don't think he ever really spoke to anyone else about what happened.

"I didn't get to see him as often as I liked when he first went to Parktown, but after I moved back to my parents, for a while I saw him every weekend. I never saw any change in him for the worse when he was at the school. He's always been the kind of child who, no matter how hard life pushes him, he always smiles. He's always been a friendly child. He never showed that he was depressed or that things were happening to him. Looking back, I think he hid it very well.

"I was also going through my own troubles at the time. I was in a very abusive relationship at the time with my little one's dad. He left me when I was eight months' pregnant with Collan's little brother. He dropped me on the doorstep of some people who looked after me. I had nothing. My dad wanted nothing to do with me and, after I had this baby, I went to them and said, 'Please. I've got nowhere to go. If you guys don't take me in, I'll be sleeping on the streets.' My dad did eventually take me in, but I was confined to my room. I wasn't allowed to take my new baby outside; my dad didn't want to see him – he didn't want to see me. It was very traumatic, but then at least I could see Collan. Every weekend I went to see him and that was very nice. And after my mom died, my dad changed a lot. Now he loves all of my kids very much.

"Much later on, I got involved with somebody else, also very abusive, and I had to call Collan – by then he was already out of Parktown Boys' – and say, 'Please, please come … He's attacking me.' Collan was studying at the time, but he came straight away. He was always very protective of me and his sister.

"I actually had my little one in prison. I was also in Sun City, like Collan was, once. I shouldn't have been there; it wasn't my fault. The guy I was with at the time, he had drugs with him, so when we got pulled over, because I was already pregnant, he gave them to me and said they wouldn't search me because I was pregnant and I was, like, okay fine. But the police officers were ladies and they did search me and they found the stuff on me. I was like, really? I'm pregnant, why would I use drugs? They locked me up. I couldn't get bail because I didn't have a fixed address – because my dad didn't want me to live with them – and you had to give them one. So I was in jail until I called my parents who finally came to see me. I had my baby in there, so they came to see the baby. They didn't get me out though. No one helped me. My mom brought me money and told me she couldn't look after the baby because she was very sick. She had cancer by then. Eventually, the police dropped the charges and I was released. That man cost me so much. He cost me my relationship with my kids – it was because of him that I couldn't look after them any more. I had to send my daughter to her dad and my son to my mom.

"But I think I'm very strong. I always thought of my kids when I was inside. They are the reason I'm still alive. If it wasn't for them I would have ended it long ago. I had to stay strong for them.

"When Collan was arrested, my dad called to tell me. I was busy working and, because I've been arrested before, I know what that feels like. I know what goes through your mind. I just kept telling him, 'Just be strong.' He told me why he'd been arrested, that there was a video of him playing 'Man of Muis'. That's what he told me. I know, I was also once in high school, so I know how kids are. I know the way things go, so I said, 'Okay, fine.' I didn't expect it to get so huge. I think it was blown totally out of proportion. Even my dad said, in his day boys always used to grab each other all the time. That's boys. Boys are boys. But we really didn't expect it to be this hectic. With the school, I just think to myself: they employed him as a coach and they never said to him he wasn't allowed to do those things in the pool with the kids. Those were all the same things done to him by his coach – he didn't know they were wrong. He's such an innocent child – he saw himself as being their age. I've got a photo of him and those kids and some of them are bigger than him; 15- and 16-year-olds, but they are huge boys. It's not like he was playing with little kids. They were his age – well, practically the same age – and practically his size."

I've wondered a lot since then what I would do if my son were ever convicted of what Petro's son had been. Did she really believe that Collan was innocent? He had admitted in court to a huge number of offences – she couldn't think he was without guilt? Could she?

"When I heard all the charges, I couldn't believe it. The problem was the lawyer made him plead guilty to all those charges and I think that he shouldn't have done that, because it wasn't true. Most of those charges are made up. If you have to ask someone, tell me all the bad things about me that you can, of course they're going to blow everything out of proportion, and that's what happened. He pleaded guilty to things he shouldn't have pleaded guilty to. I was very, very upset. And I was upset with myself because I should have tried harder to get him a proper lawyer. I know that was my fault. I had some money but it was obviously not enough and I still get angry with myself that I didn't have enough to get him better representation.

Once he'd admitted to those things, that was that. Done and dusted ... You can't take it back.

"I tried to be strong for him. I used to go and see him in Sun City and every time I came out from seeing him, I was broken. I'd cry every time. Now he is so far away, it's very hard to get there. The other day he called me to tell me there was a scuffle in the prison and I said, 'My boy, please just walk away, just walk away. I understand it's frustrating, but just be calm. I know that it's horrible, but just be strong and walk away.' He wasn't hurt but, you know, people step on each other's toes and they push each other's buttons to get a reaction out of them. I could hear when he spoke to me that he was really, really down. He kept saying, 'Mommy, I miss you. I really, really miss you.'

I need to make a plan to go see him soon. The problem for me is my little one. He is only nine years old. I haven't told him where his brother is. He thinks Collan's overseas or wherever. We don't really want to tell him; he's battling in his new school a bit. It's difficult; he's trying to adjust. We have him seeing an occupational therapist to help, but I don't want to add more pressure to this poor child. He misses his brother. He loves him. When he speaks to him on the phone he will cry every time.

"At the trial, I was lucky not to get the same abuse as Jolene. No one knew I was Collan's mother. I don't look like I'm his mother; I look much younger so people in court thought his aunt was actually his mom. The newspaper and magazine people came looking for me at my work, but I didn't want to talk to them. I asked them at work to please send them away. I did have my dad and my brother for support. I think my dad is hanging on to life just for Collan. He loves his grandson.

"One thing I noticed is how this has changed Collan; before this happened, he would always come up and give me a hug from behind; he would touch my shoulder or my arm whenever he was with me. After the trial started, he totally changed. He would never come and give me a hug; he would never come and hold me.

"I think the worst day was when I heard the sentence – 23 years! I almost died, because I didn't expect it. You know, everybody kept saying that they thought the judge was on his side. And when I was there, it really sounded to me like he was on my son's side.

"I didn't see Collan on the day he was sentenced. I didn't go to court. I thought, no, they're going to postpone again and maybe I will see him then. I was broken when I heard. Jolene phoned to tell me and then I saw it on the news. The next time I saw him was when I went to go visit him in the prison.

"When he went to Sun City, I knew what he was going to go through, because I know what I went through when I was there. I thought, my poor, poor child. When I was there, I kept myself to myself and I had my little one, Collan's brother, there. My mom had this little secret journal that she wrote in, and she often wrote about Collan. The thing I will never forget ... She wrote that no matter what I, as his mom, did, he would always defend me tooth and nail. He was loyal to a T. No matter how many times I didn't see him, he loved me. He still loves his mom. And I love him.

"Collan has such a beautiful relationship with his siblings; my daughter even has a tattoo of his name. And my little one adores him. He is such a softie. I just can't wait for him to get out and put all this behind him and get on with his life. But not 20 years from now. He doesn't deserve to sit there for 20 years. I just pray every day that they can appeal. As soon as they can do that, the better.

"I cannot wait for him to come out. I'm in a very happy place right now with a man who looks after me so well. We were dating 23 years ago and he knew Collan when he was a little baby, but we broke up. Now life has brought us back together and we are so happy. He's an angel. He says when Collan comes out he will have a job. The day he comes out he will have a place to stay and a job. He says he will look after Collan. He'll be perfect to look after the business because he's such a good person. Collan is an angel. I want happiness for him. Happiness and freedom."

Later that night Petro sent me a picture of herself, her young son and Collan, proud in his school uniform, wearing his half-colours blazer. She captioned it, "Me and my boys seven years ago today. I was so proud of my child's achievements in waterpolo. I never expected a sport that he loved so much to ruin his life like this."

But I don't think it was the waterpolo that ruined Collan's life like this. And Luke Lamprecht agreed with me.

"I have to try to be a little bit compassionate and fair to him, because I do believe there are reasons to be fair and compassionate, because he was also a child. You know, he wasn't a child under the age of 18, but the adolescent brain goes up to 25 years of age. And the fact that he could not bring himself to tell me, while I was cross-examining him, who did it to him or who taught him this, means he's still keeping the secret. He knows who those people are."

"Would that have any bearing now?" I asked.

Luke nodded.

"For sure. If he would give me a name or names, I would follow up hard. The problem is that Collan needed to go to jail. He needed a custodial sentence for lots of important reasons. But if we go back to 2009, that in my mind was when the whole homophobic story appeared. But nobody addressed the sexual stuff then. They only addressed the physical abuse. They sent me videos of one teacher lining boys up at the board, and hitting them, and then teaching other boys of their age to hit them with cricket bales, cricket bats. The boys who didn't want to hit hard, got hit harder, with this teacher standing, presiding over this. They addressed that in 2009, because corporal punishment was and is illegal. But because of the secrecy and homophobia, the sexuality thing was like a stain. Maybe if they had dealt with the sexual stuff then he, Rex, may not have been who he is today."

"But if he won't say anything, then how do you prove that?" I probed.

"There is no doubt in my mind that it was done to him. Although I could find nothing in his primary school or high school records, I could find it nowhere whatsoever, but I still think it happened to him, and he's still following the code of silence."

Luke had one more thing to say.

"I do have one question though: Where is Waterpolo South Africa or Athletics South Africa? Where is sport in all of this? Because school sport is quite something. Many sports, for that matter, when it comes to boundaries and taboo violations, sport automatically violates boundaries. You touch people and are close to people in situations people would never normally be in. The deviance comes in with the 'win at all costs and shut up about it' approach and the accompanying aggression. The boundary and taboo violation then come in, as we saw with Collan Rex, where he said that that is what he was taught at school, where he says the boys were told to grab their opponents' genitals, told to do this to put the opponent down. So when he told me that was what he learned in waterpolo, I have to ask who taught him. And where is that coach?"

Chapter 19
The Boy Who Didn't Tell
Isaac

"Hi, Sam, it was lovely speaking to you, but there's more I need to tell you. But I feel I can only talk about it if I'm in the right place. Do you think we can meet at my old school to talk?"

I had spoken to Isaac earlier that day. He had come over and sat with me for an hour while his mother went for coffee up the road. He had asked if he could see me alone because he thought it would be easier. I spoke to his mom to check that she was okay with it.

"Absolutely! I'm just so happy he's talking about it," she said. "He doesn't usually like to talk about it."

Not for the first time I wondered what had caused these boys to want to speak up now, this time. I suspected Enock Mpianzi's death had a lot to do with it. Sharon and Jonah had been traumatised by the Grade 8's death and Seth's mother had contacted me on Seth's behalf as well. Although the tragedies were vastly different, the grief and guilt were not.

Isaac was very handsome in a typical clean-cut senior schoolboy kind of way. He was tall and graceful and, again, athletic. He didn't have the same easy way with words as Ben or Patrick or Jonah. He was very cautious, choosing his words as though it was the first time in a long time that he had had to use them. The conversation started as usual, with how he found himself at Parktown and what Grade 8 was like, but for Isaac, his experiences were quite different to those of the other boys. For a start, he had enjoyed the Grade 8 camp.

"Yeah, getting up at 4am and having to do fitness sucked a bit. But the rest was great."

"And the matrics? And the initiations? How was that for you?"

"My old pot was like the best person ever actually. He just did nothing

185

but help me and he didn't do anything bad to me. Look, the matrics at the time would come and play fight us, but it was nothing brutal, nothing that left marks on us."

I was surprised and I didn't hide the fact. This was the first time I had heard from someone who had enjoyed the experience.

"So you liked it? The school and the hostel?"

"Ja, it was good ... I had a lot of fun. Through the whole year basically until ..." He trailed off.

"Until?" I asked.

"Until the incident happened."

This was also different. Most of the boys, like Ben and Seth, talked about multiple incidents of varying degrees of severity. This boy, though, had clearly suffered a specific traumatic experience.

"Didn't he touch you all throughout the year? I got the impression it was pretty much all the hostel boys," I wondered aloud.

"Well, obviously, throughout the year there were things that happened, like there was initiation, and then there were like sexual things that you had to do like he would grab your private parts and make you whistle, and other inappropriate things, but he was always smiling so when third term came ... he, like, basically built up my trust and he made me, like, really trust him. And then he took advantage of me ... One night he took me to his room and then tried to force, like, oral sex on me and stuff."

When we went through to Parktown later, Isaac took me around the school. We walked through Foundation House where most of the molestation had taken place, in the common area and in the dorm just off the room. He showed me where Collan's room had been. The same room to which he was invited to make hot chocolate on the night of the incident.

"Did you think he really just wanted hot chocolate?" I asked, leaning against the wall of the prep room.

"No," he grimaced. "I thought he wanted something else, but I still went because ..."

"You hoped you were wrong?"

"Yes," he nodded. "I was scared. So he tried to do it to me ... Then, after that, like, my year was kind of ruined because all that was on my mind was why had it happened to me. I kept on trying to erase it from my mind, but every time I did, it would stick to my mind. I was 14. I was shocked that it happened; like, I didn't think anything like that would ever happen, and then it did. I would think that it would go away if I pretended it never happened, if I pretended it was okay.

And then everything was just normal after that."

Just normal? Nothing about this was normal. What kind of normal did Isaac mean?

"So that didn't happen again, but the other stuff continued?"

"Yes, in prep, like, when we used to do homework and stuff, he always used to make me sit in front; like, he would always want to play 'Man or Mouse' – you know that game?"

I did. I wish I had never heard of it though.

"So if he puts his hand on your leg and says, 'Man,' if you say, 'Man,' he goes closer to your privates. If you say, 'Mouse,' he lets you go. Every prep lesson he used to do it, and do it, and do it. And then he used to make fun of me because I always said, 'Mouse'. Eventually, I said 'Man', and as soon as I said that he just grabbed my private parts. And from that day he grabbed it; I got a weird feeling in my body. From that moment I knew what he was."

"Could you talk to anyone?" I asked. "A friend or your mom?"

"No, I couldn't. I was embarrassed; like, I thought maybe it was my fault, that I let it happen and people would judge me."

"It wasn't your fault." I couldn't help it. So many of them wondered what they had done to make it happen. I felt desperate for them. No one asks for that. No one.

"I know." His voice was barely a whisper.

"None of it was your fault. And I don't think you could have prevented it. Do you ever ask yourself that? What I could have done to make sure it didn't happen?"

He looked down.

"Yes."

We carried on walking around the school. He took me through where the Grade 8s used to sleep and I saw where the housemasters lived – directly below those rooms. I wondered how none of them had heard these children shouting and crying in the night when they were dragged out of bed to go stand in the quad in their underpants in the cold. I wondered if they were just very heavy sleepers or if they had known all the time.

Isaac showed me the showers where Rex had often joined the boys, where the matrics had dragged Patrick and others to stand under the cold taps for hours at a time to teach them respect for the rules.

"Nothing ever happened to me here."

We went to the windows that looked down on the road, where the police van had parked and where Robert and his friend had watched Collan climbing into the back of the van that drove him away.

"Did anyone come to talk to you about it?"

"No."

His answer was short.

"Did you go to Mariolette to ask her about it?"

"No. I was originally going to keep quiet and not say anything, but then he mentioned me in his bail statement. Then ma'am obviously knew that there was much more, a much deeper thing that happened because I didn't want to talk. And then, like, I told the police officer a few things and each time ma'am knew that there was something worse that happened. She just kept pushing me until I told the police officer. It was frustrating because I didn't want to speak to him at all about what happened. I felt like Mrs Bossert didn't really care about how I was feeling; she just wanted the truth to come out. But I know she did care, but ... like, the way she did it – she could have handled it a bit better."

I wondered how I would have dealt with that if a boy I knew had been molested but didn't want to talk about it. Would I have pushed him to make a statement? Or would I have kept his counsel and let him fly under the radar until he was ready to talk about it, even if that meant keeping it from the court case? Of course, once she knew, the matron had a legal obligation to disclose. But legal and emotional aren't always good bedfellows.

"When you'd made the statement, did you realise that that meant you'd have to testify in court?"

"Yes, and I didn't want to. Nothing had come out about me at the time of his arrest and, in fact, throughout 2017, nothing came out ... 2017 was probably my best year. I was recovering and stuff. Look, I was very angry – I had a lot to process. Then in 2018 I had to tell the police officer what happened and that made me even angrier."

"Did you tell your mom?"

He looked across the school fields. It was a lovely late-summer afternoon and the sun was playing off the stands. A group of boys played touch rugby at one end and another set chased each other further off. Up against the backdrop of the Joburg skyline and the warm red brick of the school walls, the scene was as innocent and secure as you'd hope a school setting to be. Nothing bad could happen here, in the sunshine, on the AstroTurf, with boys milling around.

Looking at Isaac, I thought, this is the kind of boy I would have wanted to be: tall, confident, good looking. You'd never know what he had been through, or what the walls would tell you if they could talk. He looked bitter.

"No, I think Mariolette told my mom, but my mom wanted me to tell her, and I didn't want to do that either. And since then, I don't know, it's been tense with my mom. It broke half of my trust by making me tell her something that I wasn't ready to tell her at the time. And I've held a grudge since then actually."

"I'm so sorry." My heart just broke for this boy. For his family.

"Ja, I don't actually have a good relationship with my mom because of that ... Or Mariolette, because Mariolette forced me. Also, like, after Mariolette forced me to tell everything to the police officer, I just became really rebellious in the boarding house for that whole year. In a way, it just seemed like they weren't conscious of what was happening, and how it would affect me. They just wanted me to tell them everything so that Collan could go away."

And Collan had indeed gone away.

"And when it came to the court, they told us what would happen, but they didn't take us through it before; they didn't prepare us for what was going to happen, or for the questions. And they definitely didn't tell us that there would be people watching us on the screen."

"I thought they weren't supposed to be able to see you?"

"Well, they said that it was going to be in a room, that no one was going to see us, we weren't going to be able to see them, that we were on a television in the other room so they could see our faces and everyone could hear what we said. I saw the TV while I was speaking. And I heard my voice on the audio box next door."

"Were you scared? I would have been scared."

"No, I was just angry that people were hearing my personal story. Oh, and Collan's attorney, him and I ..." Isaac shook his head. "I was in the room for much longer than any one of the other boys because I was taking him on. Because he kept trying to change my words and make as if I was lying, and then I would take him on again and provide facts. It was like kind of a dog fight between his attorney and my information."

He laughed a little. We were back near the dining hall now. All the way down from the school hall and around the field, his story had been punctuated by the word 'ma'am' muttered all around us as we passed other boys. I had forgotten that tradition of so many boys' schools – that you were expected to greet with 'ma'am' as a sign of respect whenever you pass a woman. So that part of school manners and tradition was still alive and well.

"Is there anything else you feel I should know?" I asked Isaac.

He was on guard instantly.

"Like what?"

"I'm not asking for details, I promise," I reassured him. A lot of boys were wary that I might try to trip them up. "I mean, from a school perspective."

He gazed over the field.

"I think that's it," he said, sounding slightly surprised. "I don't think there was anything more to say."

"That's okay, it really is." It really was.

"I'm sorry," he said. "I thought there was more, but there actually isn't."

"Maybe you had to come back here to realise that," I suggested.

"Yes, maybe I did."

He started across the field. He had been recognised and some of his old friends were running up to him, calling his name in excitement: "Isaac! Isaac!" His face broke into a grin and I caught a glimpse of what he was like when there was no Collan Rex and no court case and no abuse. Just a carefree teenaged boy hanging out with his peers in the late-afternoon sun.

And my heart broke a little bit more.

Chapter 20
The Boy Who Stopped Playing
*Tyler

Three days before my deadline, Mariolette called me. "Sam, Tyler wants to talk to you. He wants to speak to you about Collan for the book."

My first reaction was panic. I had 72 hours before I was expected to submit a completed manuscript and I was worried that I wouldn't have time to do the interview, transcribe it and then write it up.

"Is he sure?" I asked weakly. Tyler and his mother were still severely traumatised by what had happened. He had suffered at school, during and after Collan's tenure there, and his mother had been on the receiving end of a lot of abuse when she had tried to mobilise other parents to speak out and challenge the school on its handling of the situation. I had approached *Julia towards the end of 2019 to ask whether she would talk to me. She had been very reticent back then.

"Sam," she said cautiously, "I would like to talk to Tyler first. I hope you understand that he cannot handle too much more. We would like to make a difference but not at the expense of his wellbeing."

I understood completely. There were boys I had deliberately steered away from because of the mental and emotional trauma they had suffered in the immediate aftermath, as well as their continuing battles to cope and make some kind of sense of what had happened to them. I only wanted to talk to families who were comfortable talking to me.

In January, Julia got back to me.

"Hi, Sam, I'm happy to talk to you, but Tyler will let me know how he feels. He is quite traumatised again, given the new disaster on the same camp that he was brutalised at."

And so Julia and I made a plan to meet and, over breakfast, she showed me a picture of Tyler: tall, good-looking, a typical teenaged sportsman.

"Look at his eyes." She was crying. "They are dead. My boy's eyes are dead."

It had been over three years since she had got the call to tell her that Tyler was one of the victim boys. She was as broken as if it were yesterday.

"We're how many years further down the road? Tyler is still exhibiting eight out of the ten signs on the post-traumatic-stress scale. He sits in his room; he stays up all night. He doesn't come out and have dinner with us. He won't go anywhere with us. For all intents and purposes, he's gone, Sam ... He's gone."

My second reaction to Mariolette's call was concern that Tyler had been pressured into talking to me. She dismissed it immediately.

"He's in the car with me now ... You can speak to him."

"Hello, Tyler," I greeted him cautiously.

"Hi there."

"Are you sure you want to do this?"

"I'm sure."

There was a long pause.

I wasn't sure. He seemed to be a man of few words so far, but so are most of the teenage boys I've spoken to and it's only in person that they open up – and even then only when they want to.

"I'm sure."

Two days later we were sitting next to the fish tank in my study. He was reserved, just as he had been on the phone.

"What are you comfortable telling me?" I asked.

He shrugged.

"Whatever you ask. What do you want to know?"

I wanted to know a lot. I wanted to know how another boy was molested for almost a year with no one knowing. I wanted to know how he was now. I wanted to know how far behind him he has put it, or whether – like another of the victim boys – he wakes up feeling or tasting Collan Rex. But Tyler's so quiet and so vulnerable that I don't know how to start.

We both look at the fish tank. There is a red fish in the tank, I've no idea what type. I got it because it was pretty and I called it Flames, because his fins and tail are long and frilly and very impressive when he's swimming. Flames isn't a major team player when it comes to showing off; his main activity up until now has been hiding under a large rock and occasionally slipping out to eat. That day, however, Flames decided to show up.

"My word!" I was stupidly excited. "He never comes out! Never."

Flames swam a figure of eight and shimmied up to the glass to peer out at us. His fins swirled like a ballgown.

Tyler leaned forward and looked at him.

"That's cool."

He was smiling.

"Maybe you're a lucky charm!" I said.

He looked shy but he was still smiling.

"I hope so."

The ice was broken.

"So ... a lot of the boys have told me that the sexual stuff became normalised, in the same way the brutality was. And that the brutality started at the Grade 8 camp. And that the sexual stuff was an extension."

Tyler nodded in agreement.

"What you just said was spot on, but it was so confusing that someone who was a master and a teacher, a coach, was doing this. You didn't ever think that a person in charge would do something that was so wrong. So I never viewed it as wrong or questioned what this guy was doing. I only noticed how bad it was when he fought one of the boys in my grade and this other guy fought him back and I thought, well, if this boy is fighting back, there must be something wrong."

Over and over, I was hearing this.

"From camp you start thinking everything is normal. You just adjust because you think, well, this is what my life is now so I'll just get on with it." Tyler looked at his hands. "I still have scars from the push-ups."

"Did you have a decent old pot?" I've seen that the ones who were treated better by their old pots felt more secure about the system. People like Patrick and James despised and feared it.

"I had head of hostel at first and life was okay, but he used to give me a lot of shit the whole time about stuff I didn't get right. One day we went to dinner and he and my [soon-to-be] new old pot were sitting there and I said something along the lines of, 'Well, at least his Grade 8s like him.' And so he switched me over to the other matric and the other guy was cool, but to get to him I had to go down to the hostel where all the matrics were and that's where stuff got rough, because although my matric hardly hit me, this guy would hit me way more."

"Why?" That seemed bizarre. Surely only your alleged mentor could hit you? It struck me that, on some level, my mind had switched into this system where being hit was okay as long as it was your official "hitter".

"No reason ... I'd be on my way to class, in hostel, and there were a few like that, who went round just hitting us every day for no reason – they were really bad. They hit us just because they could."

"You were very sporty. Playing waterpolo at the time?"

He grinned. "I did all the sports."

"Were you happy?"

"At Parktown?"

"Well, yes."

He nodded: "I was very happy. Very, very happy."

"Even though you were being smacked around and stuff?"

"I just thought of it as part of it and I had to get used to it. And I think I did, unfortunately. But even before I went, I knew what it was going to be like. My cousin was in the school before me, and he used to rough me up a lot. He told me what would happen there, so I wasn't shocked, but it was still awful.

"It was constant and stressful, because it's coming from people who you want to like you, but you ask yourself, what's the point? You have to decide if it's worth even seeing this person's face if you're just going to get hit.

"And it was every night. My matric's room was at the end of the hallway, so I had to walk past every other matric's room to get to him. At that time, any of them could call you in to do anything so, literally, walking down I'd get stopped at least three times every night."

"What would they ask you do to?" I asked.

"There was one guy who was starting a business so I had to go in and cut his cheese so he could make toasted cheese and sell it."

I laughed. I couldn't help it. He laughed a little too.

"And then in the morning I had to get my old pot's shower ready, warm the toilet seats for other matrics, get him dressed, stuff like that."

"Were you ever asked to do anything sexual?"

He shook his head. "No, nothing like that. He never pushed that."

"What was going through your mind at the time?" I ventured. Others had been terrified. Some had blocked it out completely. Still others had come to accept it. I wasn't sure in which category Tyler fell.

"My mindset was always just to get them to like me, because I thought that if they liked me they wouldn't hit me. I got pretty close to that as it got closer to the end of the year. Then one day they took all the Grade 8s and arranged them in a line from how stupid and shit they were to how super cool they were. They made this one kid go lie in the gutter, and then they put me and this other guy in the super cool section and I thought at the time, I'm here but I'm still

194

getting hit almost every single day."

"Did it get better when you moved to Grade 9?"

Tyler looked away.

"No, because now it was coming from Collan."

Naturally, the conversation turned to talk about the no-rules waterpolo.

"We thought it was okay because he would get in the pool and we thought he was showing us techniques that you could only see under the water. But then it would be so much rougher than you thought and you'd be fighting for air and realise that this is not a joke. When I was stressing about drowning underwater, it wasn't funny."

"When did it go from being half-drowned in the pool and become sexual behaviour?" I needed to be absolutely clear in my own mind on that transition, and to gauge whether the boys were too.

"At first it would be hitting and then, a month into him living there, he didn't have skaam to grab people's private parts."

I looked at him. Should I tell him?

"You were the one he brought up with me in prison. He was upset when he heard you were upset. So I got the impression that, for whatever reason, you were important to him."

Tyler looked rueful.

"You know, that doesn't surprise me. I always thought that if he was thinking of people he would be thinking of me and Jonah. We spent the most time with him. Because it was two hours' training with him and then back to hostel, so the full day would be with him."

"What was your relationship with Collan Rex like?"

"I saw him as a mentor. He was always pushing me to be better, to go for Gauteng trials. He liked me. He would ask to hug me and not in a sexual way, but like a big brother. He would always say, 'I love you,' or hug me, and I kind of saw it as him being a mentor but also a friend. A lot of people took him for quite an idiot."

I agreed. Collan seemed more instinctive than cunning. I never got the impression from either the boys or Rex himself that he had plotted it as a long-term strategy.

Tyler nodded.

"I agree with that. I think exactly the same. He started getting more and more into it and no one ever stopped him. I wanted to stop him though, every time.

"I can't remember the first time with me exactly, but I know stuff happened in the pool with us. It must have been when we would have to swim up and against him and try get around him in water-polo ways and he would start grabbing at you. Yeah, I think it started there and then he came to hostel.

"He would do the same thing: he'd hit you, he'd grab you down there and ask you to whistle. I didn't think it was okay. It was annoying having to look out for it." I could sense the bitterness in Tyler's voice. "Everywhere I went I was constantly looking out for him or for matrics, because then I'd either have to dodge or get hit for no reason or get told to do something and all three I wasn't keen for.

"It was quite depressing. And it really hit me when Jonah left. It was really hard. Because the whole time, from December until January, we were talking about how the next year was going to be so cool and then January came and he wasn't there. He said, 'I'm sorry, I didn't know how to tell you.' I couldn't speak to him for nearly four months. It was so rough, because I was dealing with shit in hostel and I thought, now I have to do all this alone ...

"The sexual stuff was confusing and upsetting but I just thought that's how it has to be with Collan. I was always worried he was going to do stuff like that to me, but I carried on like nothing was happening."

He looked so sad.

"Even in court, they asked me how many times something happened and, to my mind, it happened every single day. Being with him and talking to him and having that type of stuff happening was very hard and very off-putting, but at the same time I knew he was trying to help me with waterpolo. It was my goal; it was what I had my heart set on, and he was pushing me towards better teams even though I thought I couldn't make it. I thought, this guy really sees something in me, he knows what he is talking about and he's mentoring me, and two minutes later he was hitting me or grabbing at me or walking past and just punching me for no reason at all."

"Did you ever tell your parents exactly what happened to you?"

"My mom knows more than my dad and even she only knows I was being hit and groped from day to day. I think the first time my dad knew anything was when they read out the charges in court."

Court. Where all the boys had been traumatised again. Tyler agreed.

"It was hard in court because I knew for a fact he could see me."

"I thought he couldn't?"

That was news to me. The Palm Ridge Magistrate's Court is one of the few courts in the country where children could testify out of sight of the defendant. I already knew from James that the cafeteria

196

was a free-for-all, but I was sure that once the children were in the room in which they testified, they could be confident that the defendant couldn't see them.

"That's what they told us. But they could. You're in a room where the glass is one-sided, but when the lights are on you can see right into it and I could see he was looking exactly at me. It was really stupid."

And really frightening for some of them, I was sure.

"I don't feel hatred. I just want to forget him. I never think about it. These are the only times I think of it."

"I'm sorry."

"No, no ... There's been good that's come from it. I'm more emotional now; I understand emotions better. It gave me a chance to change Parktown in a way. Because it happened to me, and that was the first time something like that was coming out, it was a chance to show that the school isn't what they think it is; it's not this amazing school where boys go to turn into men, which is what I thought it was. It's actually a shit place. I always had a bad feeling about it. I was always walking around worrying about who was next to me, who was around me, who was gonna see me ... It was a shit place."

Tyler was angry. He was the only one who had shown such anger.

"I left the school because I was done with it. It wasn't the place I came into – the respect wasn't the same. Obviously, I didn't want what happened to me to happen to other kids, but no one cared about respect any more. I went from stressing, walking through a door without looking to see if someone older was behind me, to walking past a bunch of Grade 8s all giving me this look of 'Who are you?' I went through all that shit in order for it to be like this now. And I missed home."

"Home was a safe place." He was nodding.

"You know, I wasn't even there when he was arrested. I think one teacher had threatened to cut all my hair off so I caught a bus home, but the next day everyone was talking about it. I didn't know exactly why he had been arrested; I remember hearing that he was forcing himself into kids' rooms in the Grade 9 section and later on I heard they saw him on camera wrestling me."

"It wasn't you," I shook my head. "It was Jonah on the tape. And it wasn't wrestling."

I told him what I knew and how Collan had been caught on camera doing a lot more than wrestling. And I told him about Ben and how he had decided to do something about it, and that's how the Bosserts saw the tape.

"It was guaranteed to happen," he said. "He was always in the common room." And then the surprise: "What was he like in the prison?" Tyler asked.

"He's not in great shape. But he's found God and he does a lot of outreach in the prison and he's done a few Bible courses. And he says he's very sorry he hurt you – you, in particular."

Tyler was interested.

"God can forgive you ... I think I've forgiven him. There's stuff I hold against him, that constantly gives me trouble. [But] the fact that I know now he understands it and to know he's religious makes it a bit better."

I fetched my laptop from the desk.

"Would you like to hear about what he says about remorse?"

"Yes please."

I read this piece to him.

"I'm an alcoholic," I said to Collan , "and one of the things you're supposed to do as part of the 12 steps of recovery is to make a list of anyone you've harmed and, where possible – where to do so wouldn't cause greater damage – to try and make amends."

He nodded.

"Is that something that ever goes through your mind?"

"Of course it does," he said.

"I did feel remorse. Because of my bail conditions, I wasn't allowed to contact any of the boys or anyone at Parktown, so for me to tell them I was sorry was difficult. When the judge said to me I hadn't shown remorse I was like, well, how can I? I told them in court I didn't mean to hurt them; I didn't want to hurt any of them. With all those attempted murder charges, I said in court I didn't mean to kill them or hurt them. I didn't ever want to hurt them. I didn't."

"If Tyler was sitting here now in front of you, what would you say to him?" I asked.

"If I could speak to Tyler now? I hope he could forgive me and that one day he could find healing and this doesn't overwhelm his life. All those boys saw me as their friend and I hurt them; the way I've impacted their lives caused a ripple effect and I know that. After I got arrested I met one of the boys from the waterpolo club and he told me that some of the victim boys were taking drugs and fighting and getting out of hand. And I didn't want that to happen to their lives."

He talked about this on the phone as well. "I am sorry for hurting them. I don't want their futures to be affected. I actually really wanted them to prosper in waterpolo. Some of them were really good players. I wanted them to do well. And I'm the one who probably took their love away from that sport, or even hurt them to the point they don't want to play any more, so that hurts, because I know how it feels. Because my passion was waterpolo, coaching, refereeing, playing, all of it – now I can't do that any more. So I understand I took away a passion of theirs and I never wanted to hurt anyone in that way."

Tyler nodded.

"That sounds like him," he said, and then looked away. "I don't know, hey. I don't know how to feel towards him."

Neither did I.

"How do you feel about yourself now?" I asked.

"I'm upset with myself that I didn't see that it was wrong, that what he was doing was wrong, and I'm upset that I didn't stop it."

"You couldn't have stopped it," I said.

"Maybe I could have. And when Enock Mpianzi died I felt like I should have said something earlier."

"How would that have changed what happened to Enock?" I said.

"If I had spoken out about the Grade 8 camp and the stuff we had to do there ..."

I shook my head.

"What happened with Enock was a tragedy. And nothing you said would have prevented it."

Tyler didn't look convinced.

"How would you, talking about how you were bullied and hit on camp earlier, have stopped a child from drowning?"

I told him what Luke had said. How the Harris Nupen Molebatsi report had shown that the stories told by the children and the educators had backed each other up. How it was the camp's story that Peter Harris dismissed as rubbish. I told him that during the activity that took Enock's life the matrics were busy planning how this camp would be the start of the new Parktown, and how they were working with the hashtag #itstopswithme.

"Nothing that happened to you happened on that camp," I said. "So you coming out earlier would not have saved Enock's life."

He was quiet.

"That makes me feel better. It really does."

"Trust me," I said, "Don't try to bear more than is yours. There are a lot of things in life you will feel guilty about. Don't make this one of them. There was nothing you could have done to prevent this."

There was a faint smile.

"Is there anything else you think I should know? Anything else you'd like to tell me?"

"It's taught me a lot of stuff; some stuff you can't just learn, you have to go through the experience to understand. I question everything now. I don't just accept what people tell me. I work it out for myself."

Chapter 21
The Boy Who Lost His Life
Enock Mpianzi

Getting hold of people in authority is always tricky, and it proved to be even more so in the writing of this book. I had a plan. I was going to talk to all the boys first. Then Collan and his family, and then teachers, the school governing body, and the MEC, in that order.

My rationale was that once I had the stories of the victims, I would be able to speak to Collan and ask him about himself and about what the boys had told me in relation to how he remembered things, both with the victims and with the boys who had, in turn, molested him during his own school years.

I then approached some of the teachers whose names had come up regularly in my conversations with the boys and their parents and, to some degree, with Collan. The only one prepared to speak on the record was the former Director of Sport, Remo Murabito, who had by then left the field of education. I had sent him and two of his former colleagues the same message:

"For the past few months I've been researching and writing a book about the Collan Rex case, and about how vital traditions and bonding experiences in a boys' school can be damaged when someone goes rogue, and can change the whole ethos of a school known for over 100 years of tradition and excellence."

I suggested to each one a chat over coffee and said that if afterwards they would prefer not to be involved, I wouldn't badger them. The other two were still in the education field. I met with one who, as was his right, declined after our meeting and received a message from the other telling me he would rather stay out of anything to do with Parktown.

I was disappointed, but unsurprised. I still had requests lined up to send to official bodies, and towards the middle of January those were ready to be sent. I wanted to gain some closure for the parents. All of them felt they had been let down by the authorities, by the school itself, the education department, with some feeling that the MEC had used the case to grandstand, that he didn't care about the boys or their parents and that he never had.

Then Enock Mpianzi died. It was awful, the worst thing that could have happened and I was reminded over and over of one mother's anguished question to me during our interview: "Does someone have to die before anyone takes this seriously?"

Well, someone did. And under the most horrific circumstances.

In early February I gave everyone breathing room, but with my March deadline looming, I started approaching different stakeholders for answers and comments and personal feelings. I started with the busiest of all, the MEC for Education in Gauteng, Panyaza Lesufi. I'd always been a big fan; he was usually the first MEC on the ground when there was a crisis, so on 21 February I sent an interview request via WhatsApp to his spokesperson, Steve Mabona.

I was very clear about what I was looking for. I told him what the book was about and what I wanted from Mr Lesufi: "I feel his perspective is essential and his obvious pain over it all touched my heart. It's clear he works tirelessly and I'd like the book to bring that across."

On 24 February, I reminded Steve of my request. He asked that I send him an email. So I did.

Dear Steve,

I hope you are well. We actually spoke quite a few times when I was at 702! You very kindly organised the MEC for several interviews. As I said in my message, for the past 6 months I have been writing a book about the Parktown Boys' molestation case, in the words of the people who were there at the time. It's not an exposé, or a shock factor book. It's about the feelings and actions of everyone, from the boys, to their parents, to some of the teachers.

I would very much like to talk to the MEC for the book; it would be incomplete without him. I feel that his perspective is essential, and having watched some clips of him at press conferences at the time and meetings, his feelings and pain come across strongly. I think in many ways the media has been unfair to him; it's clear he works tirelessly and is very hands on and I'd like the book to bring that across in his words. I reiterate, it is NOT a tabloid-type exposé.

I would need an hour with Mr Lesufi and I will fit in with whatever he can manage. The book deadline is in a few weeks; the short notice is

not deliberate, I just know he has had a really tough start to the year.
  Look forward to hearing from you.
  Warmly,
  Sam

By 5 March I'd had no email response so I WhatsApped Steve again on 9 March. Then again on 10 March. He asked whether I had sent an email because he didn't remember seeing one. Luckily, I had both the mail and the read receipt to show him and he assured me he would attend to it. I messaged him again on 11 and 12 March, then sent on 16 March another email, which was also read, begging for a response.

Dear Steve,
  I hope you are well and taking care of yourself during this difficult time. I desperately need your help. I am on a very urgent deadline and as things stand will have to go to print without the MEC. This means I will have been turned down by the school and the MEC for any kind of input and it will look terrible. I've approached Kevin Stippel who approached the GDE with no response and I know that Malcolm Williams is off limits because of his suspension.
  I have a book full of parents desperate and angry because they say the MEC doesn't care and never has. I don't believe that. As I've said in WhatsApp messages to you and as per my previous email, I believe very differently about Mr Lesufi, and think he is given a raw deal regularly by the media.
  If he is not meeting people any more because of the coronavirus and is worried, then here are some questions he could answer in writing. I don't think it would take long.

· *What goes through his mind when he thinks about the tragedies at Parktown? How does he process?*
· *How does he manage when he's trying to balance the emotions of parents with the long-term survival of the school?*
· *He said in a press conference outside the court during the Rex case that the reason he hadn't released the full Harris Nupen Molebatsi report to the parents was because he was concerned about the names of educators and children being exposed, especially if someone left the report lying around somewhere. The parents say he is hiding it because either he doesn't care or he's afraid of a lawsuit. How does he walk that tightrope?*
· *He arranged to have a matron, Mariolette Bossert, in the boarding*

house which improved it instantly to, probably, one of the safest and nicest in the country. Are there other measures he is considering?

- *Can Parktown survive this?*
- *What keeps him getting up and going to work every day in the face of all this pressure?*

The latest I can push this out to is Thursday morning. Then I have to submit the manuscript. As it stands, it will go to print with no official comment whatsoever. Please please, can that not happen? Please please can he add in the value I know this book needs from him.

Regards,

Sam

On 17 March, Steve responded, assuring me that he had forwarded my request to the MEC's office. At time of submitting the final edit, I was still waiting for a response. In the meantime, a journalist friend had given me the MEC's personal number. It rang out. I left messages but … nothing.

I also approached former headmasters of Parktown. One was initially very open to an interview, but then withdrew from any involvement with the book and asked me to delete all statements he had made. I am still unsure as to why. The current headmaster, Malcolm Williams, also declined my request.

I also contacted the Parktown Boys' school governing body for an interview. The SGB is either loved or hated, depending on who you talk to. Some former members had told me that it was just an Old Boys' club with no care for the pupils. The Archivist didn't agree. "I think they need to bring on more people who have the solutions to the problems," he told me over coffee. "That school is easily fixable – you just need dedicated people to get stuck in and do it."

"Would you want to?" I was curious.

"Yes, absolutely," he said. "There's so much good to be done there. You just need people who will roll up their sleeves and do it."

I contacted Jim Pooley from the SGB and he promised to put it on the agenda of the next meeting, which he kindly did. The members decided that while they would not participate in an interview, they would send me a statement.

Dear Sam

The SGB has given careful consideration regarding the interview offer for your forthcoming book.

We have come to the decision that we would like to give you a factual statement on the issues and the proactive steps that have been taken in the best interests of the learners, both past and present. We will not be putting anyone forward for an interview.

Here is our statement:

"*Parktown Boys' High School is in the process of healing from painful incidents in its past.*

"*The school today serves a diverse community and its student population has risen to approximately 75% from previously disadvantaged groups. It is consistently rated as among the best performing government schools academically and extramurally in South Africa and we know that our diversity is our strength. The school was 50% oversubscribed for the 2020 academic year. Our focus is Values-Based Moral Leadership which helps ensure that we develop good husbands, good sons, good fathers and good brothers who will make a difference in their school, in their communities and in society as a whole.*

"*In April 2018 a new School Governing Body (SGB) took office, including nine volunteer parent members and in August 2018 a new headmaster joined the school to refresh and accelerate the changes required to the school's processes, structures and culture. Over 50% of the teaching body was changed in 2017 and 2018 which has significantly advanced our culture change programmes. Gauteng Department of Education (GDE) MEC for Education, Panyaza Lesufi, has said Parktown Boys' High School remains one of Gauteng's best schools.*

"*In November 2018 a judge's sentencing of Collan Rex, a Waterpolo coach and former hostel master at the school, to a total of 23 years for sexual and common assault charges marked a watershed moment at the school.*

"*The school has implemented recommendations contained in the Executive Summary of the Harris Nupen Molebatsi Attorneys (HNM) report into the Collan Rex case commissioned by the Gauteng Department of Education (GDE). The school has also regularly employed the specialist advice and input of Mr Rees Mann from the 'Male Survivors of Sexual Abuse' organisation and Mr Luke Lamprecht, a leading Psychologist and Child Safety Expert who advised the school following the REX report.*

"*The recognition of our progress is shown in the support of our parents, our school community and the significant increase in applica-*

tions to the school for the 2020 school year. We remain consistently oversubscribed as boys wish to be at our school.

"The Nyathi Bush and River Break camp tragedy in January of this year that resulted in the death of Grade 8 learner Enock Mpianzi has shaken the school to its core and the school is still a place of mourning. The SGB and the school [have] pledged its absolute support and commitment to the GDE and the South African Police Service (SAPS) investigations into the tragedy at the Nyathi Bush and River Break camp. We remain utterly committed to playing our part in ensuring Enock and the Mpianzi family receive the justice they deserve.

"What some of our boys went through in the past can never be diminished or forgotten.

"The school is determined that these tragic events will never be repeated. There continues to be an unrelenting and shared focus on the process of healing, learning and advancing transformation that we have embarked upon to forever change our culture."

I showed the statement to the Archivist.

"Wow." He sighed. "They really have an opportunity to do so much good, you know. I don't understand it."

He looked at me.

"What are you going to do?"

"Publish it," I said. "Put it in the book as is."

The irony of it all was not lost on me. The very teachers who had insisted that there was no code of silence, the educators who wanted everyone to work together – as long as they didn't utter a word outside the gates – and the MEC, who had spoken out at the memorial service for young Enock Mpianzi, entreating the learners to break the code of silence, was himself, at least in this case … silent.

It left a bitter taste. How could this school have any chance of changing when the very people entrusted with the lives of these children were themselves sticking to their own code of silence?

According to the official report, Enock Mpianzi's death had been the result of negligence at the hands of both educators and the Nyathi Bush Camp where the orientation camp had been based. From the time the buses, filled with over 200 children arrived at the camp, the trip was characterised by a series of errors. The roll call list of the children attending the camp was left on one of the buses, and the boys went straight into a water-based activity: raft building. The boys, split into groups of 12 to 15, had to build a raft to transport one of their members across the Crocodile River. Many of the boys couldn't swim and there were only 12 life jackets available. The river was swollen after the summer rains and when there was a sudden rush of water, no one was prepared, especially those who should have been. Boys went flying, some dragging themselves to safety, others relying on other boys and camp facilitators to rescue them. One news report describes some of the boys who had made it to the relative safety of an island in the river as being told to get back into the water because, as the current was so strong, the faciliators deemed it too dangerous to get in themselves. The boys were told to float downriver where they could be more easily rescued. There was no buddy system in place, the boys didn't know each other, so when Enock disappeared, there were few voices speaking up that he was missing. The list from which the headmaster had to work was of all the Grade 8s, not all of them at the camp, so when individuals didn't instantly respond to their names, assumptions were made that those boys were safely at home. The search for Enock only began the day after he went missing, and Mr Williams – in an effort to discover which boy had disappeared – phoned his parents to check whether he had actually gone on the camp. I cannot imagine the horror those parents went through, to receive a call from the head of a school, one who was supposed to protect learners, asking as to the whereabouts of their son.

The death of Enock Mpianzi stirred up a lot of feelings for the parents of the boys who had been abused, for the new parents, and for parents who had tried to support the school throughout the past few years.

After Enock died, businessman Rams Mabote, himself a former teacher and parent at the school, wrote an open letter to Malcolm Williams, the headmaster of Parktown Boys' High School. Rams is well known in media and his voice is a powerful one. At the time of writing, he was using it for 'Future Kings', a programme run by his foundation to provide mentorship for young men from underprivileged backgrounds.

Dear Mr Malcolm Williams
  Headmaster: Parktown Boys' High School

It has been a week from hell, hasn't it? But if that's how you feel, imagine how the family of [Enock] Mpianzi still feels now, a week after his demise.
  You do not know me, Sir, so let me tell you who I am. I am a social

commentator, a journalist, a PR coach, I am a mentor for teenage boys and an advocate for responsible manhood, and most importantly I am a parent of a boy at Parktown. And I am writing to you mostly in my capacity as the latter two, but certainly in all the stated capacities.

Like most parents and all those associated with the school I was hit by shock when the news came out and a part of me hoped it wasn't so. No one wants their school or the school of their child to be in the news for such reasons.

I still gave you and Parktown the benefit of the doubt. Accidents happen, I reassured myself. It does not mean that I did not feel sorry for [Enock] and his family. Why, like most parents I heard that voice that kept on saying "it could have been my boy".

Right from the beginning, you and the school handled this matter very badly. If reports are anything to go by, you kicked for touch, were not forthcoming and wanted to hide behind the excuse of "let the law take its course". The same way as the school was seemingly negligent with the boys on that Nyati Bush and River Break camp, so it seems you were flippant in communicating to us, the school community and the country at large. In fact, "flippant" is a euphemism for something stronger and unprintable.

And then, Sir, you had the audacity to invite parents to the school on Monday only to tell them not to ask questions. What the hell? What was the point? To feed them your propaganda without accounting? Mr Williams, even a junior PR person could have told you to take the questions and rather be evasive or non-committal in your answers. But don't treat adults as sheep to the slaughter. That you can do it with the learners doesn't give you any licence to do it with their parents. You lost credibility for this.

As if that was not enough, Parktown has been on a roller coaster of very bad PR. The stories have been inconsistent. The goalposts have moved. The contradictions too many. And blatant lies told. I mean, to lie to the media that [Enock's] family could not afford a life jacket when in your memo to parents – which is now public – no one was required to bring their own, and no one did. That was low, Sir, very low. In the process you compromised The Sunday Times, who to my surprise bought your bad spin lock, stock and two barrels and were left with egg on their face.

I did not think it could get worse, but it did. And then on Wednesday on Radio 702 a letter written by one of the boys who went to this camp and had made the acquaintance of [Enock] was read on air during the Eusebius McKaiser Show. (Let me pause to say Eusebius [and 702] has done an amazing job for not only keeping the story alive, but also for diligently asking all the questions on everyone's behalf, following up on every possible angle of the story and most importantly, of giving [Enock] a face, a name and posthumous dignity, which it would seem the school and the camp could not afford him.) In the letter the unnamed boy states clearly that he informed the teachers immediately and several times more subsequently that [Enock] had been swept down the Crocodile River, but he was ignored and almost ridiculed.

Even when I thought we had reached rock bottom, it went down even further. Now the camp has released a statement which actually has contradicted so many of the "facts" that you had told us in the past seven days or so. They threw you under the bus. They blame you for late-coming, for not doing roll calls when they were supposed to be done. Well, you seem to corroborate them because by your own admission, you called the Mpianzis on Thursday (long after [Enock] had clearly drowned) to ask them if their boy had come to camp. Sir, I cannot find anything more morose.

Here is what I think is happening, Mr Williams. To me, this is a classic case of toxic masculinity. A boy disappears (and later dies) and all the men in charge of the boys agree in a brotherhood of silence and a conspiracy of lies – if not by commission, certainly by omission. Subsequently, you are reported to have beckoned the boys to not speak about the incident. How tasteless! You asked the boys to participate in a conspiracy of lies, secrecy and deceit. Is this what you are bequeathing to our boys? Are these the leaders you are preparing for tomorrow?

Mr Williams, I had faith in you as you came in during the horrific waterpolo boy-grooming episode a few years ago. You seemed upright. You seemed to want that past to be erased and put the school on the right path. I was impressed because even during that saga, Parktown had gone under, secrecy was the code. Our boys were made – perhaps subtly threatened – not to talk. My own boy, who was then and is still participating in waterpolo now, said little. I believed him when he said he was not a victim of the beast that was subsequently sent to jail. But I still felt he was not forthcoming. Now I know he was just following the instructions, the culture of silence, lies and deceit.

Sir, I believe Parktown is a good school, that is why I have kept my boy there. I love the spirit of brotherhood, especially during sport, *win or lose. I love the school band, the best I have seen in Gauteng. I love how black boys are given opportunities in sport and to become prefects, even though much more can and should be done. I think these traits can and should be copied by most public and private schools.*

But sadly, Mr Williams, South Africans are beginning to associate Parktown with crisis and grime, bad culture and poor leadership. We live in a country where men have and continue to terrorise and destroy society through rape, abuse, murder, theft, corruption and greed. It is very sad to send our boys to a "good" school, only for them to be taught the very values most of us hope to undo.

Whoever you are protecting, Sir, whatever you are not telling us, please know that in his death, [Enock] deserved more, he deserved the truth, even if it is too late. You should have done better. You can still do better.

Yours sincerely
Rams Mabote
Father, Mentor

I called Rams to ask whether I could publish his letter in my book.

"Of course you can, of course!" he said warmly. "Tell me about this book."

So I told him. I told him of damage and breakage and sadness and guilt and attempted suicides and fractured families and a system designed to protect only itself.

"This book needs to come out," he said.

"What made you write that letter?" I asked. "Were you angry with the school?"

"I was angry with the silence. Yet again parents were being told nothing. I wanted change. I wanted a response. I didn't expect my letter to go viral."

I laughed, slightly bitterly.

"Well, I bet you got a response after that!" I said.

"No," he said, "I never did."

I was horrified. The letter had been picked up by media outlets, both print and digital; it had been discussed on talk shows, at dinner tables and certainly within the school itself.

"He didn't contact you personally after it came out?" I was astounded.

"Sam, no one contacted me. Not the school, not the Department, no one."

They had all ignored a man with a very big voice.

"I even emailed Mr Williams personally," he said. "I offered help. I said I would do whatever I could."

"And?"

"And nothing."

I felt sick.

"You know what I've realised?" I said sadly. "That when I started this book, I wanted to find the rogue in the system."

Rams was quiet.

"But there is no rogue in the system. The whole system is rogue."

He agreed.

"Write this book, Sam. I want a copy."

Chapter 22
Consequences
Collan Rex

The second visit to see Collan nearly didn't happen. I had to travel for four hours back up to the prison to drop off the interviews we'd done together and the chapter on him, so that he could read it and be sure I hadn't made any factual errors. I didn't trust the postal system, and I couldn't leave it much longer – my deadline was only a week away. Jolene had a church function on the Saturday so I offered to take her with me on the Sunday. She hadn't had another chance to see him since our last visit. I set my alarm again for 2:45 am.

Then Jolene texted me.

"You know Limpopo is on lockdown?" she asked.

"Limpopo is not on lockdown – only the place where they are keeping the people who came back from Wuhan."

About 130 South Africans had been trapped in the town of Wuhan, at the epicentre of the coronavirus pandemic. COVID-19 was, by early March, sweeping the world and South Africa had about 34 confirmed cases, the "Wuhan South Africans" bunkered down at a resort called The Ranch.

"Limpopo doesn't have a single recorded case," I said. "So I'm going."

"I know, I'm just scared."

She seemed so young and in need of reassurance.

"We will sanitise all the way there and back, take minimal bathroom breaks and keep all stops very short."

"Okay, then let's do it."

Jolene had straightened her hair this time – there would be no repeat of last time's feud over hairclips.

"I'll put my face on later," she said, clambering into the car in fluffy slippers. She caught me looking and gave me a brilliant smile.

"Don't worry … I brought shoes!"

I wondered how she kept up her happiness for these visits. So short and so public. And so far apart.

"And best you behave yourself," I said. "Or I'll drop you off at The Ranch; it's only two kilometres off our route."

She laughed. She was excited to see Collan.

When we got to the prison we sat in the car and I read her the 19 pages I had printed off for Collan to approve. It took half an hour. Afterwards she was quiet.

"What do you think?" I asked cautiously.

She thought for a minute.

"Ja, it's good. It's the truth."

"Well, if you like it, he'll probably like it," I said, more hopefully than I was comfortable feeling.

She laughed.

"Possibly!"

We followed the same procedure as last time: signing in, depositing money into his tuckshop account, and then handing over the pages. The guard who was in charge of what the prisoners could and could not receive was curious.

"What are these?" he asked, flicking through the pages.

"It's a story about Collan. For him to read," I said.

He looked up.

"A story of Collan? Why?"

"I told him I would." Seemed weak.

"Is it a nice story?"

That was a tough one.

"I think it is a story he won't mind being told," I said cautiously.

The guard slipped the pages back inside the envelope.

"What must I write here though?" he asked, pointing to the book of receipts. He had to fill in what I had brought so that I could give it to Collan to check once he received his parcel. Prisoners only got their stuff on Mondays.

"Well, it's just ... a story of Collan."

He nodded and wrote, *A story of Collan Rex*.

All the staff were wearing masks. We were given hand sanitiser as soon as we arrived. I couldn't help but wonder what would happen if a visitor brought the virus into the prison, knowingly or unknowingly. It would be a death sentence for many.

As soon as we reached the visitors' area it was immediately clear that everything had changed, it felt different. Jolene was different too. She was very quiet and seemed edgy. I knew she was concerned. In the car she had told me that Collan had had to be moved from his block because another prisoner had unearthed an article about him and what he had done. There was a scuffle and both he and Collan spent five days in lockdown.

As soon as Collan came through the door I could feel the tension. He was puffy and his skin was sallow. He looked very tired. I asked him if he was okay. He wasn't.

"I know how women feel now," he said. "Everyone is just looking at me like I'm a piece of meat."

I didn't know what to say to that. I thought lots of things though. About how the boys had felt when everyone found out what had happened to them. And I worried that something would happen to Collan now that people knew who he was.

There was an awkward silence.

"So … I have some good news, or news that I hope you will think is good news."

He looked slightly suspicious.

"Ben would like to come and see you," I said. "He wants to tell you he has forgiven you."

Collan was aghast.

"Of all of them, he was the last one I ever thought would want to do that."

"Well, he does," I said. He nodded slowly.

"Would that be something you would like or be prepared to consider?" I asked.

"Yes, of course," he said. "I just … I can't believe it."

"Which part? That he wants to see you or that he wants to tell you he has forgiven you?"

"Both."

I could see Collan had been thrown off balance. I pressed on. The visit was only two hours and I wanted to give Jolene and Collan as much of it alone as I could.

"I have some more good news," I said.

"Yes?" he looked less suspicious and more hopeful.

"I spoke with Luke Lamprecht this week," I said.

His face clouded over a bit. He didn't have happy memories of Luke. The last time he had seen him was in court and Luke was very firmly on the side of the state.

"Yes?"

"He told me that if you want, he will come here and you can give him the names of the people who did this to you." He shook his head.

"No, I won't do that. I can't."

"Why?" demanded Jolene. "Why won't you do that?"

"Because it will ruin lives," he said.

"And your life isn't ruined?" I said.

He was resolute.

"One day I will get out. And then I will be with Jolene."

"That could be years away," Jolene interjected. She was upset.

"Please tell him thank you, but no. I won't do that to people."

I was frustrated and so was Jolene. This was something that could make a real difference, not just to Collan, but to everyone who had ever been too afraid to name their rapist or abuser. That damned code of silence was alive and well in a prison in Limpopo.

I changed the subject.

"I spoke to your mom this week," I said.

The old Collan resurfaced.

"She said so! How was she?" he asked eagerly.

"She misses you," I said. "And she says she loves you very much and can't wait to see you."

He looked rattled.

"I miss her too, and my little brother. We talk on the phone when she calls and sometimes he cries."

Jolene stood up and headed off to the bathroom.

"She's the most wonderful woman, my mom," he said. "Everything she ever did, she did for us."

"What are you going to do ... now that people here know what you are in for?" I asked.

I couldn't help but worry for him.

"I'm in a new block now so it'll be fine," he said. He leaned over the table and whispered. "That guy at the table next to us? He's been here for 14 years. He's serving three life terms."

That guy at the table next to us looked like he wouldn't say boo to a goose.

"For what?"

"I don't know," he said. "You don't ask that kind of thing here."

But someone asked about you, I thought. What would happen to you now?

When I got home, there was a Facebook message from Ben. He was online when I opened it.

"Did you tell him about what I said?"

"Yes, I did."

"And what did he say?"

"He said he would like that very much. I don't think he believed me though – he was very shocked."

"Why?"

"Because he said you were the last one he would ever have thought would want to see him again."

"But I do though."

"Are you sure you've forgiven him?" I asked.

"Yes, I am. I forgave him a long time ago."

"Wow," was all I could manage.

"So when I get back we must organise it."

I promised to help him do exactly that.

That night, due to the spread of coronavirus and the implications, President Cyril Ramaphosa declared South Africa to be in a State of Disaster. All prisons were closed to visitors for at least 30 days. We would be the last people to see Collan Rex for a long while.

Collan called me on the Tuesday morning.

"Hi, Sam."

"Hi, Collan, how are you doing?"

"Better today. Yesterday I wasn't feeling well."

"I'm so sorry to hear that," I said. Had he read the extracts from my manuscript yet?

"How are you feeling today?"

"No, much better."

"Did you have a chance to ...?" I began but he was already talking.

"Yesterday I read it and I was very angry."

I gulped.

"Okay ..."

"But today I read it again. And you've been fair. It's the truth." I could detect the sadness in his voice. "I couldn't expect you to be completely on my side."

I felt a rush of sadness myself. For this broken boy and for all the boys who were broken because of his brokenness.

"Collan, you know I think you are where you need to be," I said. "I've told you that. But I also think it's very wrong that you are the only person in jail; I think you need psychiatric help and 23 years in prison isn't going to get you that."

"Yes ..."

"And I've tried to show who you are as a whole person."

217

"And I can see that. So thank you."

There were a few errors he wanted corrected and I promised to do that.

"Besides that, do I have your approval?" I asked.

"Yes," he said again. "It's the truth."

Epilogue

By the time this book went to print, no one had been criminally charged, despite the recommendations outlined in the first Harris Nupen Molebatsi report of 2018. Education spokesperson Steve Mabona spoke to *TimesLIVE* at the time the findings of the report became available and stated that all those implicated would be charged. Almost two years later, there have been no further developments.

Some 18 months later, several of those teachers named in the report are still working in the education system.

James's dad, Michael, received an email from the school to tell him they would no longer be paying for James's medication or psychological care.

The Harris Nupen Molebatsi report on the death of Enock Mpianzi was damning. It found that both the teachers and the lodge were liable and that disciplinary action should be taken against the teachers for negligence and recklessness.

The headmaster Malcolm Williams was still on suspension, following the findings of the Harris Nupen Molebatsi report on the death of Enock Mpianzi. So he was only suspended 4 months ago. No other disciplinary action had yet been taken against him or anyone else at the school.

Collan Rex remains in a maximum-security prison. He will be there for another 22 years.

Acknowledgements

This book could not have been written without the help, support and honesty of a veritable team of people.

To all of the victim boys and their families, thank you for talking, some of you for the first time, and allowing me to tell your stories. You are the bravest people I have ever met.

To the experts who gave of their time, answered countless questions with patience and kindness, and offered extra resources – your contributions give this book the context it needs.

To all the educators who spoke to me both on and off the record, thank you for the information and the perspectives.

This book wouldn't be what it is without the tireless, kindly relentlessness of Melinda Ferguson. No one else could have pushed me through this as efficiently and as brilliantly as her.

To Sean Fraser, the best editor I have ever worked with, thank you for not sleeping for days in order to do this book the justice it deserves.

For my family and friends, thank you for the love and support. This was a tough and traumatic time and for those around me I am profoundly grateful for your understanding, every time I write a book. I promised my husband this will be the last one for a while. He patted my shoulder, rolled his eyes and said, "Yes dear."